A Legitimate Journey

Navigating Grief and Trials in the Light

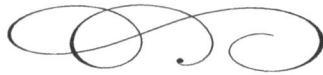

A Legitimate Journey

Navigating Grief and Trials in the Light

KATHLEEN D. HAMILTON

Henschel
HAUS
publishing, inc.
Milwaukee, Wisconsin

Published by HenschelHAUS Publishing, Inc.
www.henschelHAUSbooks.com

ISBN: 978159598-583-5
E-ISBN: 978159598-584-2
LCCN: 2018930067

Printed in the United States of America

Dedication

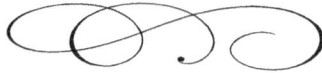

To my children who constantly teach me the meaning of love: Kristy, who had to weather the greatest tempest of my tears and her ability to radiate laughter; Bryan, whose pure and innocent awareness of his sister's presence helped me understand the light; Carrie, who arrived on the wings of her sister's love and has continually held me up with hers.

To Joe, whose love has kept me warm so I could write this book.

To Diana, my spiritual sounding board, for her loving encouragement.

Ayden, Forrest, Ricky, Porter, Trison, and Gracie who remind me that God continues to bless our future.

To Randi, who exemplified the true meaning of friendship, and last, but most definitely not least, my Savior and Redeemer Jesus Christ, who has carried me through my journey, and my Heavenly Father whose love is shown to me through every ray of his warming light.

Contents

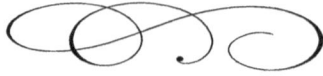

Acknowledgments

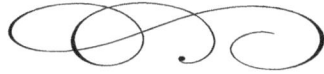

I must acknowledge God with deep appreciation for continually tapping on my shoulder about the importance of sharing my story. Without his continual promptings, gentle whispers, and guidance through my trials, this book would not have been possible. Sharing my story is the least I could do, considering that without his light and love, I would still be floundering in the wilderness.

My love and appreciation to all those spiritual giants who were brave enough to blaze new trails of understanding and whose wisdom has illuminated my path to appreciate the masterpiece of my heart and soul: Gary Zukav, Dr. Wayne Dyer, Deepak Chopra, M. Scott Peck, Stephen R. Covey, Steve D' Annunzio, Betty J. Eadie, George G. Ritchie MD, Jaquie Davison, Joel S. Goldsmith, David O. McKay, Duane Crowther, Albert Einstein, Max Gerson, Charlotte Gerson, Norman Fritz, Carl Jung, Buddha, Benjamin Franklin, George Washington, Maya Angelou, C. S. Lewis. There are too many to name, but I love and thank you all.

I want to thank those who reached out in love and compassion during sorrowful times, and those who stood and cheered during happy ones. To Dale and Sherida who faithfully showed up with love and compassion in the beginning days of my sorrow and witnessed with their lives how the light really works.

Introduction

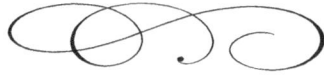

I didn't sign up for the race I found myself in when sorrow arrived, but when the gun sounded and I took off running, I had no idea how long it was or what the prize for finishing was going to be. I didn't see flags or markers to direct me or clues to locate them, but I was running at full speed. Partway into the race, however, I discovered it wasn't a race at all, but the beginning of a long journey—my spiritual journey through grief.

There are many who have not been faced with being spiritually lost in a wilderness, adrift at sea, or tossed about in a turbulent storm, but at some point, every life will know some kind of wilderness only to discover that a compass or map to lead them back home could possibly save their life. The ways of suffering are innumerable and unique, but the goal is to make it home safely. If we turn away to hide from the pain, we remain stuck or we hinder our healing by missing the miracles that show up to help us navigate to safety. Knowledge is valuable as we seek to understand affliction.

We come to this earth with a preordained purpose and an appointed time to return home. We learn to love and then we learn to say good-bye. When the time comes for a loved one to leave, it may seem like the end of our world because loss is diminishing—as it should be, but we can't control the timing or the circumstances, only what we choose to do with them. Each one of us has a road to travel to experience the challenges, feel the pain, and recognize the joy—all of which will refine and mold us into the graduating students of this earth school. Each journey is an individual one and some may choose to drop out, fail, or avoid the lessons, but it is not for anyone to judge the outcome of their choices. I do not consider myself an expert on the subject of death and grief. I am merely a student of experience, yet the more I experience and the more I learn, I recognize the truth and purpose for it all.

A Legitimate Journey

The world is collectively suffering tragedies and grief more than ever. It is frightening because grief can be collective and, if not dealt with, can morph into even greater afflictions. In one way or another, we are all affected. Grief comes in many forms, not only death, yet the further we move away from truth and our spirits, the more we suffer. We are also becoming more enlightened and the knowledge of healing is obtainable more than ever, so we don't have to be lost at sea if we choose not to be.

I want to share my journey in hopes that it may inspire others to find the light that will lead them to discover their purpose and start their healing. Just for a while, I would like to be the driver of the grief bus and point out some paths to healing or lighthouses on the shore.

My grief, time, great teachers, miracles, and learning how to see and feel the light gave me a story to tell, and I will do it by recounting experiences, sharing excerpts from my journals, and sharing the lessons I have learned. Every time I hear a story of someone starting on the same journey, my heart swells with compassion because I know what they will need to be able to survive, but I also know that if they embrace the light, they will not only see the tip of the iceberg on the surface, but the mountain underneath.

We often read in books that grief can be a teacher, sorrow can refine us, and time heals wounds, but we don't actually get the map that tells us how to get from point A, suffering, to point B, healing. I've read many books by authors who have great clinical observations of grief, but no personal experience, so there are some things they just don't understand. When one thinks of all the things that can throw someone into pain, there isn't one book or one set of rules that apply to everyone, but there are many who have traveled the road that can help you steer clear of some of the potholes, deadly cliffs, and dangerous mountains. This book is not intended to present myself as a victim of unfair adversities, but to acknowledge tireless armies of heaven and angels standing by to help, to instruct, and to sustain me in my darkest moments, giving me the courage to be a victor and not a victim.

I give credit to my Heavenly Father and his loving grace for the message in this book. He is leading me with his light so that more of his children will know of his love, feel his compassion, and know how to reach out and seek the warmth and sustaining power of his light—he loves us all! Ask your heart if this is true, and trust what it will tell you.

For everyone that asketh receiveth; and he that seeketh
findeth; and to him that knocketh it shall be opened.
Matthew 6:8

Mountains, like dragons tower incredibly high,
Challenging our desire to sadly scream "why?"
But to move it, you must scale it, even with pain,
For it is in ascension,
The challenge will recognize the gain.

Climbing Mountains

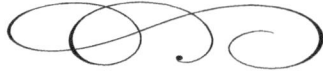

If it were possible and I offered you a chance to step into my shoes, crawl into my skin, or see the world through my eyes, you would probably politely decline the invitation, if for no other reason than the assured fear of the unknown. I can tell you how I feel, I can share my pain, but without walking in my shoes, seeing through my eyes, and living in my skin, you always have the option to turn and walk away. It is human nature to turn away from pain. We don't ask for it, we don't seek it, and we try to run like heck from it.

When we stare up at mountains, we are being challenged. When we find ourselves in a wilderness, we feel lost. When we are tossed about in a turbulent sea, we are confronted with fear. At some point, everyone will face a mountain, a wilderness, or a turbulent sea, and it won't be so easy to turn and run because that is grief, and until we deal with it, count on it following us like a shadow or holding on like a boa constrictor.

How do we find our way back home in spite of those mountains, those wildernesses, and those storm-tossed seas? If life drops us in anyone of them, how can it drop us back into victory, joy, and healing? It is possible, but it does take work. When you realize the truth of the matter, that life can be difficult, that everyone will face challenges, then accepting it makes transcending them possible. When you find yourself stumbling through a series of problems in shoes that only fit your feet, you can't expect someone else to step in and walk the walk for you. Sometimes, just knowing others have worn similar shoes, made the journey, and survived to tell about it can inspire you to rise above your challenges—I am one of those others.

It's hard enough to climb mountains, let alone have the strength and the faith to move them. I discovered moving a mountain without a miracle though, is incredibly difficult. Over the course of thirty plus years, I've stared up at mountains that appeared insurmountable, ones that towered over me like fire-spitting dragons, yet like threads of gold, those mountains weaved themselves into the fabric of who I am. Every spurt of fire, every painful event, and every peak became my teachers.

This book is about finding my way back to joy and victory in spite of those mountains by learning to view them through fresh lenses, new paradigms, and opening up my heart to deal with the pain. It is also about recognizing miracles, then showing up to do the work of healing.

I was the third child of six—I married at eighteen, fresh out of high school with dreams of being a perfect wife, a loved daughter-in-law, and of course, a mother. I also had the noble aspiration of being perfect and making my parents proud, so my course was charted. There was no doubt in my young mind that it was time to launch my boat and sail through life on the calm waters of perfection, believing in God and viewing the world the way I wanted it to be.

My father, a veteran of World War II, met my mother when she was thirteen, then at sixteen; he talked her into eloping to escape the dysfunctional life that had become her existence. Both of them had endured lives of abuse at the hands of irresponsible parents and aunts and uncles who had a tendency to abuse alcohol or be involved in sexual exploitation. They were both emotionally and spiritually wounded people when they found each other, but fortunately, they had a desire to end the cruel cycle of abuse with their cherished union. It was a marriage made in heaven—so I used to hear, but how did they know of heaven?—neither had ever experienced it. It only made sense when missionaries knocked on their door in 1958 that they embrace the gospel of Jesus Christ with eager hearts and willing spirits. They had faith; it could raise them above their past and give their children a better life. It took courage to smooth the stone in which their lives had been etched, but with Christ in their lives, they gathered the courage and began a new life.

Because of my mother's childhood, she held her children close to her heart, sometimes to the point of suffocation. Perhaps it was a guarantee that we would not stray far from the path of virtue or fall into the murky pit of sin. Yet, I think she believed the wounds on her soul could heal by rearing righteous children, ignoring her pain and forgiving her perpetrators, so for those reasons, she permitted her abusers to stay in her life and around her family, and as her children, we were required to have tolerance for them all.

Mom was an angel, no unkind bone existed in her body, and she loved her children more than life itself. Her nature was calm and gentle, and it was my safest aspiration to be just like her, even though I was just the opposite—feisty with a will of iron. I didn't know the entire story of her childhood until after she passed away—then things made sense. I was convinced she was a master of disguise. She hid the smudges and suffered in silence like a pro. She never talked about it, engaged in therapy, or cried. Needless to say, I believe it eroded her insides because she always had health problems, and she died young.

My father was a hard worker, but he had a hard time showing his children affection or encouragement. He couldn't hide his pain like my mother did. He was an intelligent man, yet he constantly challenged his beliefs and peace danced around him like a feather in the wind and he was never able to catch it and hold on. After Mom was gone, his anger at those who hurt her as a child grew like moss in a swamp. For them, forgiveness was not an option, and it chewed away at his happiness until he fell into a state of hopelessness.

I was a typical young girl that had to scrap my way through the confusion and mayhem five siblings created, but still I had dreams of being a ballerina, singing, acting, and finding a Prince Charming even though I felt like I belonged in the land of misfits. I was tall and lanky and towered above all the kids in school until I reached high school. In kindergarten, they ordered a special desk for me, "the monster desk" that sat at the back of the class so I wouldn't block the view of all the tiny kids. Teachers would corner me on the playground and have me stand still while they compared me to each other, always speculating that I was destined to be at least nine feet tall—like Goliath. One day, I ran home from school and wanted Mom to tell me the story of Goliath so I would have an idea what the teachers meant when they referred to it as my destiny. I had fear of such a future. I so badly wanted to be tiny and normal—my value hinged on it.

A Legitimate Journey

We come into this world pure and innocent, and before long, one step at a time, we begin allowing external things to tell us who we are, who we should be, how to look, and how valuable we are. When we are babies, we are content to observe the world from the inside out without expectations or the use of language, but as we grow, part of the world teaches us differently.

My family went to church, ate dinner around the table, and went on family vacations together. As large families go, we were pretty close. If we argued or fought, Dad thumped us on the head, and if we broke a rule, Mom put us on restriction— depending on the severity of the crime, sometimes a week or sometimes a month, but we always lived through it. We all had to take our turn doing the dishes, and on Saturdays, we couldn't play until we flawlessly cleaned the house. However, I cannot recall conversations that covered topics any heavier than the importance of making sure we cleaned around the bottom of the toilet, our skirts being too short, being nice to relatives, or being quiet in church. We never talked about death, family tragedies, sex, or even the way Grandpa tried to touch us girls inappropriately. If there were life events happening around us capable of stopping us in our tracks, we didn't discuss them, so of course, we didn't discuss how to cope with them either—but who knew, maybe no one did. Mom wanted us to see the world through those proverbial rose-colored glasses. She was all about trying to stay positive in a world that could swallow us and spit us out if we let it, so when upsetting things happened, it was best to close the curtains or sweep them under the rug.

When I was thirteen, my uncle Dell, a serious alcoholic, had a car accident and died from withdrawals in the hospital. I wanted to go to his funeral and my mother tried to talk me out of it. I threw a fit until she relented, but with a caution not to look in his casket because she was sure I wouldn't be able to handle seeing a dead body. I didn't heed her advice; in fact, I not only viewed his body but lingered, studying his hands, the color of his skin, and the fact that his lips looked strange until I was asked to move along so others could view him before the service. I thought I had time to locate a restroom before the service, so I slipped out and headed down a long hall with many doors. I stopped and gazed into one of them since it was wide open. I saw a young man with orange hair lying in a casket. He was probably about seventeen or eighteen and his beautiful casket with gold handles was surrounded by colorful bouquets of flowers. That image disturbingly stuck in my mind much longer than uncle Dell's because he was so young, and young people weren't supposed to die.

I had to admit that my mother was right, I didn't handle the funeral very well, and for a while, every night, I was sure my uncle was walking around the house and it scared me. As for the young man, his image in the casket just kept running through my mind like a clip from a movie, but I wasn't going to talk about it.

At fourteen, I met the boy that would eventually become my husband and the father of my children at a church dance. Upon graduation from high school, he served two tours of duty in Vietnam, one on a ship and the other on a swift boat. I waited like a lovesick school girl for him to return. He was wounded in action and came home with a Purple Heart and a Bronze Star. To his family and friends, he came home a hero and he relished in it, retelling his story over and over and each time, embellishing it just a bit more. When post-traumatic stress became a household word associated with war, he was sure it applied to him in a good kind of way, along with his exposure to Agent Orange. What I soon came to learn was if you didn't have an answer for something, you could blame it on Agent Orange. Confusion with the Vietnam War was normal because as young people, we didn't really understand the why's and how's of it most of the time, so we didn't know how to deal with it, but we married anyway and embarked on our journey into marriage, parenthood, and scaling mountains that were too high.

Mom used to say that some of the most important and beautiful things in life were the simplest to grasp. When you are from a big family, it helps to keep things uncluttered by keeping them simple. At least I was a child from a non-broken home, and compared to many of my friends, I was lucky. That was simple to understand, and I appreciated it.

Looking back, I was not equipped to marry at eighteen, but if someone would have tried to convince me differently, it would have been like trying to crack the safe at Fort Knox. I was headstrong and thought I knew everything that mattered. However, I had more fear than faith when it came to God. When I moved out of the house, I entered the real world and it was not so simple—in fact, it was just the opposite.

I cannot offer scientific proof about what is in this book. I have no physical evidence to prove that we all have a seed of truth in us that helps us recognize truth when we see it, hear it, or feel it, yet I can steer you in the direction of knowing this for yourself. When grief comes, it waters that seed, and there is a spirit of light that can grow if we allow it to—we aren't expected to suffer alone. If you want to know what I write is true, your truth meter will be your witness and the way to research what you read is to put it to the test.

When grief entered my life, it crashed to shore like a tidal wave moving me out of the tranquil mooring of the harbor and into the rough seas of sorrow. I not only wished to die, but felt that I surely would. My journey through those rough seas, and there have been many, is what I want to share in the following pages of this book. I didn't have the skills or the education to take any of it by the horns and look it straight in the face. Sorrows are not simple things to grasp. I had to learn step by step and line upon line.

My first consuming grief started with the death of my first child, a sweet, strong-willed daughter who crammed as much living in her years as she could. She was talkative, creative, passionate, and headstrong; she questioned and challenged everything. In the middle of her twelfth year of life, she died in an accident that totally blindsided me. I had no time for a good-bye. When she died, part of me died. Hurt, grieving, and trying to stumble through life, I seemed to be faced with one mishap after another: miscarriages, a stillborn infant, my mother's death, and the grief of a father who could not deal with his loss. When my child died, he told me to have faith and know she was with God, but when my mother died, he was angry at him for snatching the love of his life away—a loving God wouldn't do that. Yet that is grief—individual and personal. Others standing on the sideline cannot experience your pain or live it for you—yet they can't learn your lessons either. I offered a home to my father, and trying to grieve his grief and mine, I suffered a mental breakdown. I began to have severe health problems brought on by grief, and when it seemed like I had all I could handle, my young son of five slipped on wet concrete and suffered a severe concussion that left him in a coma for four days and a brain injury that made his life a challenge to navigate. Trials kept cropping up until my first marriage ended, and the family fell apart like a sand castle swept away with the tide. The challenge of trying to help my children through their grief, the divorce, and their hardships seemed more difficult than dealing with my own.

I had hope when I met someone I believed was placed in my life to help me, so I remarried again, believing I had a port in the storm, but the reality was, I didn't—I was literally tossed right back out to sea. It turned out to be a physically and emotionally abusive relationship, only to end with the betrayal of infidelity. I grieved for the marriage I had hoped it could be and for the realization that it never would be.

Even though I witnessed my relative's abuse of drugs and alcohol in childhood, it didn't protect me from the heartbreak of it with my children. Their way of dealing with grief was to self- medicate. I felt hopeless watching them destroy their health and risk their lives. Trying to rescue them was like trying to jump into swift-moving rapids with only an outstretched arm but no line to pull them to shore.

Yet there were times that I surprisingly found my head rising above the water and my lungs filling with air. I also realized that even though I wanted to die, I wasn't going to. Wishing for some quality to my life, I began to search, to study, and to seek for ways to survive. I became a student hungry for knowledge and reached for any and all evidence that could lead me or teach me to know that survival was possible. I hungered for stories of miracles and sought after those with similar experiences; I bought books by inspirational writers and prayed my heart out for the strength to get through each day in spite of my sorrow.

While searching amidst the tears, anger, despair, and ignoring my physical health, a multitude of miracles began to happen. What brought about the change? I think it was surrender but also the realization that I was exhausted trying to do it alone. If I didn't try harder to make it to shore, I knew my boat would sink. I needed to find a way to patch the holes and hold on long enough to see the miracles that would lead me to safety. Besides the death of a child, a parent, a stillborn baby, and two heartbreaking divorces, I've experienced broken relationships and a child with mental illness. I have grieved tremendously trying to help my children through drug and alcohol abuse and have grieved with a friend whose child was murdered. I had to help my younger daughter cope with the death of two school friends: one was an accident like her sister's and the other a murder. Then as if a rough childhood wasn't enough for her, she developed a brain tumor and was deserted by her husband because he couldn't deal with her illness. I have watched helplessly on the side-lines while a brother of mine and his wife's family was thrown into the heartbreak of the missing wife of their nephew, with no answers yet in sight, and we all witnessed the horrendous public scrutiny that ultimately lead to the senseless suicide of their nephew and the murder of his two innocent children. Without trying to sound pretentious or insensitive, I can quote the old cliché, "Been there done that," only to show that I have walked in those difficult shoes and understand what such journeys are remotely like to travel, still understanding that everyone's journey is a very personal one—none have a template. This book is not about religion. We are all precious in the eyes of God. Separating and scrutinizing others religions only rob us of understanding how to safely finish the race. I am a Christian, and I can assure anyone that the Jesus I love is the same Jesus they love and the God I love is the God to all the children on earth. The greatest teacher you will come to know and understand will be that seed, that inner knowing light that will witness what your truth is.

Throughout my journey, I have come to realize that we are given trials to teach us so that we may grow in the compassion and love that brings an awareness of what life is honestly meant to be. It is no shame that I have had to be helped up more than once, and there were times I felt life was picking on me or I was being singled out from the crowds.

Believing in God or thinking I needed to be perfect didn't guarantee me a life free of pain, but it also didn't mean God was singling me out because I didn't measure up either.

This has been a spiritual journey, and spiritual journeys aren't always easy and they are sometimes long, but when you take it in the light, there are rest stops along the way where joy, miracles, and laughter can take place. The thing about learning as you go is you learn to locate the first aid kit sooner and then you aspire to help others find it as well.

A detailed map revealing the perfect route isn't slapped into our hands when life presents us with challenges; we haven't all had perfect childhoods, exposure to God, and some have not been given much love in their lives, but everyone is a candidate to find their path to healing, but sometimes it requires veering off the comfortable beaten path we have become accustomed to.

When we are in a state of grief, how we view the world changes, and throughout the ages, some who have navigated it successfully have gratefully added to the map. Those who have had to wear the shoes of grief and learn firsthand what it is like are the teachers who have earned their diplomas. If we are blessed to be enlightened, we will be called to serve. Life is like that, it gives us the opportunity to either learn or teach—to do both will help us evolve to a higher state of spirituality. That, in a capsule, is the prize at the end of the race. It has been said that ignorance is bliss, but I can testify that it is not when you are grieving.

You must to be willing to die,
To be able to live.
You must be willing to fail,
To be successful
You must be willing to do that which you cannot
To do that which you can.
You must be willing to be ordinary
To be noble.
You must be willing to fear
To be courageous.
For it is knowing the dark,
That you will recognize the light.

Courage

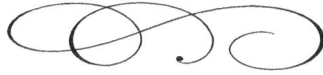

The first step of the journey through grief is the hardest—it requires the greatest amount of courage. Looking through the curtain of tears can challenge us to care about the journey, let alone muster the courage to travel it. In the beginning, there are few prepared to face it head on. Most of us tremble because we haven't experienced the kind of physical, emotional, or spiritual pain that challenges our very existence. At one time or another, all of God's children will be tested. Even our universe is constantly being tested. A lot of these challenges have resulted in weather patterns that create great catastrophic conditions resulting in a tremendous amount of human suffering. Thousands of families have faced incredible adversities that don't make it on the evening news, yet they have exemplified valiant and daring behavior in the face of them all. Who will walk with each one of those valiant?—walk in their shoes, cry their tears, and battle for the courage to survive. If no one does, it will still be enough if they do it for themselves and manage to carry on. We can't fight everyone's battles, go down with every ship, and crest every mountain, but we can fight our battles, sail our ships, and climb our mountains—and that is enough.

My sister related a story to me that made me think about our options when we believe we have none. She is a devout nature lover, and wherever she goes, she seizes every opportunity to capture beautiful photographs. Her camera is like an appendage: where she goes, it goes. One summer while traveling to visit my father, she made a quick decision to divert off the main road and take a detour over a mountain range she assumed would eventually lead her back onto the main highway. It was one of her usual habits to look for opportunities to try new routes—because if lucky, she could capture unbelievable beauty. The reason she had such a wonderful portfolio of photographs was because she did exactly those kinds of things—veered off the beaten paths! It was a spontaneous decision that day and she admits she didn't look at her map, assure her tank was full or let anyone know her plans. However, her excitement overtook her common sense and she started her trek over unknown territory anyway.

She related the story, saying it was very beautiful in the beginning, and the road was narrow and nerve-racking because there were lots of twists and turns, but she knew it was to be expected—that's how mountain roads are. She had been traveling for some time before she rounded a sharp curve and realized the pavement ended and she was on a narrow soft dirt road. She knew if she took her eyes off it for a second, she would plunge over the side; it had no shoulder, only a frightening cliff framed the edge. She continued on, however, in spite of her misgivings and soon rounded another bend only to discover it wasn't one mountain she had to get over but three. Three or a million, they loomed before her like giants with the same terrifying dirt road, deep ravines, and rocky jagged edges for as far she could see. Even then, she couldn't resist the temptation to snap a few pictures while trying to assess her situation. However, she had to admit she was afraid. She wasn't sure she had the courage to continue traveling on the narrow road, but it became very clear to her that there was no room anywhere to safely turn around. It was at that time she started to berate herself for being so impulsive and irresponsible by not checking her gas tank or letting someone know what she was doing. She had no idea how far she had to go to get over the mountains. For the first time ever, she admitted she had put her life in jeopardy.

She couldn't imagine what kind of a vehicle the narrow dirt road was designed for— certainly not a van like hers. Short of parking her van and hiking out of the mountains, there was only one way out, and in spite of her fear of running out of gas and daylight, she had to travel the road forward. She needed courage because her physical safety depended on it.

If you are on an unfamiliar journey into grief with no way to turn around, how will you get the courage to move forward? Your survival depends on moving forward and the kind of courage you will need will be the most difficult to tap into.

There are different kinds of courage, some we get because we are facing physical danger, or seeing someone else face danger and without thinking, we react. We can't always control that kind of courage, it is built into us; it assures that our species survives. Then there is moral courage. It's even more of a challenge because we have to find the courage to act when it's uncomfortable— whether we are faced with going against popular opinion or we know our consequences will be painful, yet for the good and for what is right, we know we don't have a choice. Sometimes, it requires deep soul-searching before we can determine if we are willing to pay the price.

Spiritual courage is not the same as the other types of courage, it is actually the highest form of courage and the hardest, yet it is required to rise above your grief and become whole again. The path isn't always discernibly present. It's not one you can take a snapshot of and examine. You probably wouldn't know where to aim the lens if you could because with each person it differs.

In the beginning, most people don't know how to look up, how to walk in any particular direction, or how to believe that there is a way to stop suffering. Grief is like that narrow dirt road, and there are risks in traveling it. Fear tells us it has no end, so why travel it, yet the purpose of fear is about survival, doing what we have to do to achieve it. The first step forward requires the most courage, but I say, "Stay on the road and move forward!"

It was scary, and as you may have guessed, my sister, totally exhausted, eventually hooked up with the main highway, but she was never sure at any one time how long it would take or how dangerous it could get. Yet, she had no choice. With a few prayers, honking her horn as she rounded the curves and keeping her eye on the path, she gratefully arrived, vowing to study her map better the next time, checking her gas tank, and definitely letting someone know where she was.

The road to healing lies in how we view our horizons; in this case, the word horizon means how we view what we believe lies ahead of us—how we are led by our observation or experience. Because we are individuals and we enter that road at different levels of challenge, we have to view things personally. We think we desire for the journey to be easier than it is and wish to be shown how to travel it inch by inch to assure our safety, but like turning around, it can't be done. That is why the journey of spiritual growth and healing requires courage because we are being asked to travel over uncharted territory. In this life, we are never guaranteed or shown what is around every corner or that the journey we are on has been successfully traveled by a hundred others. Geographically, as it was with my sister, we are constrained by the limits of our physical view, but the horizons that are within us are only limited by the boundaries of our thoughts or our imaginations. It is by personal experience and our courage that will decide whether we make it to the highway of healing or not. If you take the initiative and muster the courage to go forward, you will broaden your spiritual horizons and be able to see beyond those mountains.

We yearn to have definite answers and mapped out roads to our destinations, but without developing spiritual courage to call upon, we are unlikely to find those roads. This kind of courage means opening up to our vulnerability and searching to understand and have the faith that we will arrive safely in spite of the fact that we may face many rocks, terrifying jagged edges and stones that move as we step. We may slip occasionally and end up with a bruise or two but ascending mountains is not easy, however, making it to the top then becomes self-mastery, which in essence is spiritual freedom.

What is courage anyway? It is the ability to face difficulty, uncertainty, and fear without being overcome or defeated. Courage is a state of the heart and it is the ability to make the right choice even if it scares the heck out of us. It's also like a muscle: the more it gets used, the stronger it becomes.

How do we get the courage we need to survive? Sometimes, it's all about change and transition. Why is change or transition important? It is important because to travel on a road we are unfamiliar with or unsure of, we must free ourselves of old roads, old habits, negativism, and skepticism. Remember, this is your life; if you are stuck in the burdens of the past, you cannot take advantage of the present, and the present is where your healing will begin.

By having the courage to take the first step, you will begin to see that God has your back and there is divine order to everything. You may have your fears and doubts, but the main highway will eventually appear and you will have won the victory.

> *For God hath not given us the spirit of fear; but of power,*
> *and of love, and of sound mind.*
> *2 Timothy 1:7*

Know that in the stillness of asking for courage, it is there inside of you to tap into as you begin your journey. Do you long to follow your heart, to heal, to be whole, and to have the courage to begin a new path? If you find yourself at the edge of a cliff, have the faith to know that one of two things is likely to happen: God will give you wings or he will catch you if you fall. Believe that, and it will launch you in the direction of courage. It's easy to forget that we have the power to claim our life and claim our healing. Even though it exists within us, we lose sight of our wonderful fearless self.

> *Have not I commanded thee? Be strong and of a good courage;*
> *be not afraid, neither be thou dismayed; for the Lord thy God is*
> *with thee wheresoever thou goest.*
> *Joshua 1:9 (kjv)*

Before grief appears, most people are content to live complacent lives, requiring no more than the strength to avoid the snooze button and get out of bed in the morning. It's easy to insulate ourselves from failing by making safe decisions, but when your life is in danger, you usually have to ask for the courage to believe in something that is higher than yourself and asking for courage requires courage. If you are ever going to have meaning in your life, courage is the thing that will help you take your first step onto the path that leads to the main highway and out of the woods.

A Legitimate Journey

Courage is the most important of all the virtues, because with
out courage you can't practice any other virtue consistently.
You can practice any virtue erratically, but nothing consistently
without courage.1
—Maya Angelou

Courage is often referred to as someone displaying acts of bravery or her-oism. Yet on a day-to-day basis, we display and use it in our lives in small endless ways all the time. Every time we face a fear and overcome it, we are using courage. Courage is our path to personal growth. Yet no one can understand their own courage until they have had to face their own fear. Now, in your grief, you will be called upon to be your hero. Courage is the ladder that will help you peak that mountain.

Mark Twain believed that when it came to courage, it wasn't so much about lack of fear as much as it was about acting in spite of it. We all experience fear at some point, and courage is our way of mastering it.

Sometimes, just to get out of bed in the morning when your heart is broken is a pure act of courage. But every time you do it, you will gain strength and confidence to do it more. Of this, I can testify with surety. You will reach a time when you can honestly say, you have stared pain and fear in the face and have lived to tell about it.

Victor Hugo reminded us that to live through the great sorrows in life and learning how to have patience for even the small ones, we have accomplished a great task and we deserve to go to sleep at night in peace. Even the serenity prayer tells us to accept the things we cannot change, the courage to change the things we can, and the wisdom to know the differ-ence. Just believing that takes courage. Sir Winston Churchill told us that it was the courage to just continue that counted.

Just as my sister discovered on her journey, even though she couldn't see around each bend, she went anyway. Within each one of us lies the dormant seed waiting to be watered, waiting to teach us, and waiting to heal us, waiting, waiting, waiting to give us the source and the strength to continue on in spite of the pain or the sorrow.

Journal:

September 27, 1982

> *I was talking with Mom about how difficult it was to stand beside Lanette and watch her life slowly fade, but it was next to impossible to not cry even though the hospital staff was constantly warning me to control my tears. I expressed my concern over the way they handled the situation. My mom listened with heartfelt sorrow and suggested I write the story down so I would always remember how one small trace of compassion could leave such a profound imprint on someone's heart when they found themselves suddenly in need of understanding. I retired to my room and on my old Royal typewriter wrote: "A Tear for Lanette."*

A Tear for Lanette

Lanette came into the world, a bouncing 9 lbs. 8 ½ oz. She was a lively, happy, and determined child who seemed to cram so much living into every day of her life. As she continued to grow, my pride and love increased as it does with most mothers and their children. When you believe you can never love more, you always find you do. She loved music, drama, and singing. I marveled at her imagination and the stories and poems she could create. She loved babies and couldn't resist reaching out and touching their tiny hands if someone walked by with a baby stroller.

When she was five, I took her to see the Sound of Music. Then it became official, she would only answer to "Maria." She carried around a little overnight bag and said it was her guitar—no one dared tell her different. That lasted for a year. During that summer, she would round up every available child in the neighborhood, sit them in a circle on the lawn, and tell them stories. As I sat outside observing her one day, she looked over at me and said, "Hey, Mom, I am teaching school!"

All my children are beautiful, and she was no exception. As a child, I would have wanted to look just like her. I was tall and gangly with auburn hair and large freckles chaotically competing for every pale available spot on my face. She was petite, olive skinned, and her light hair glistened in the sun like strands of gold. Yet she still fought for her justifiable spot of value in her critical world. Because she was so dramatic and so full of life, kids would tease or criticize her and she was too sensitive to ignore it. She lived in pain the last year of her life, and my calling became that of her personal cheerleader. I had to constantly remind her how beautiful and talented she was. I recognized a diamond when I saw one, and she was one. As for her future, the sky was the limit. With her talent and tenacity, there was nothing that would slip from her grasp if she didn't want it to. We would sit and talk about her future and what she wanted to be when she grew up—there were so many things—how was she to choose? I could only assure her that God would lead her to know. God knew my child and loved her, but no one else knew her like I did. I was her mother, she was my child—need I say more? The bond between a mother and a child is special, and I know if I were to ask any mother about her children, most would say the same thing: how grateful they were and how special their children were. It is about love—about loving someone so much that they give meaning to your life—loving so much that every day they are in your life is a better day because of them—or the kind of love that creates hope for a future of love continuing to grow. It is that love that gives you physical comfort by just touching their hands, stroking their hair, or breathing in the essence of their being. Love; whether it is between a mother and her child, or a father and his child, husband and wife, or the love of a dear friend, it spells life—my life.

On September 10, 1982, Lanette was hit by a car while riding her bike across a newly paved road. Her friend Randi followed close behind and witnessed the scene that would tragically take her friend's life. I wasn't aware of the accident until I turned a corner on my way home from running errands and found myself behind a long line of traffic and flashing emergency vehicles in the middle of the road. As I got closer, I recognized her new bike lying mangled on the curb. My neighbor, Gayle, had been frantically pacing and watching for me, and when she spotted my car, she ran up and informed me Lanette had been hit and they had airlifted her to Scottsdale Memorial Hospital. Gayle's daughter was with her, and in an urgent command, she told her to take my other two children out of the car and to their house so we could head to the hospital. She began to cry as she got in the car, saying she had been the one that held Lanette in her arms until the paramedics arrived. Trying to speak through tears, she anxiously ordered me to drive fast because she didn't think Lanette was going to last very long. "It looks real bad!" she said, her voice cutting in and out as she trembled.

Upon arriving at the hospital, I raced in, every part of my body shaking like a leaf, and I demanded to know if my daughter was still alive. A nurse at the desk told me to go sit in a little room that sat off the main waiting room and a doctor would be down to talk to me.

A tiny room, which for a claustrophobic person like I was, seemed like a sentence to solitary confinement. I was shaking, I couldn't hold still, I kept going out and walking around, only to be told to go back and sit down. The nurse said, "We will send you the chaplain, maybe he can help you make some phone calls."

"What do I need a chaplain for?" I asked. "Is she dead?"

There was no answer. I paced for what seemed like an eternity, and finally, the doctor walked into the room and stated in an emotionless declaration, "Your child has a very critical injury. Right now, we are taking a CT scan of her brain, and when we get it done, we will be able to tell you more."

Finally, someone arrived to escort me upstairs to the intensive care unit, and I was led into another small waiting room to sit and wait. I kept asking to see my child. I had to let her know I was there—it was very important! I kept asking until the doctor finally came into the room. He stood there for a moment, leaned against the wall, and said, "There is just no way that any human being can possibly survive the kind of head injury that your child has. There is just no way."

I looked around, hoping he had the wrong room and he wasn't talking about my child, then I started trembling so fiercely I felt my insides were about to leap out of my body. I looked at the doctor, "How will I ever live without her?" I cried. "Tell me how!" I stopped, my eyes turned to saucers, "I want to see her!" I demanded stone-faced with an obstinate voice--- "Now!"

A nurse entered the room and informed me that when I settled down she would take me to see my daughter. "You need to get control of yourself!" she ordered. She repeated the order a couple more times before I realized time was crucially ticking away. As if someone had reached over and turned off a faucet, I stopped crying, wiped away my tears, and said, "Okay, I stopped. Now, take me to her room!"

When I entered the small room that barely held the gurney Lanette was on and the nurse standing next to her rhythmically aspirating her with a large bulb syringe, I asked why they didn't have her hooked up to life support. No one answered. I moved closer to see my child's beautiful face bruised and swollen; her golden hair was drenched and clinging to her head. My child, one who always had so much pride in her appearance, and there she was crumbled, hurt, and struggling for her life. I couldn't help it; I started to cry again, sensing somehow that I wasn't going to be able to bargain with God to spare her life. I could only choke through my tears, "I love you, and I am here with you." A stiff hand on my shoulder reminded me that if I was going to continue crying, I would have to step out of the room. I turned and glared into the eyes of the same bossy nurse. "Are you kidding me?" I asked in disbelief. "I am her mother—don't you know what I am losing?" She was my child; who had more of a right to cry than I did? So what if she hears me cry? I was becoming angry. Then I was taken by the arm and escorted against my will back to the small waiting room.

The chaplain came in and asked if I needed help making some phone calls. "No," I snapped. "You of all people should know that I need to be in there with my daughter. She will awake and not see me there—she will feel alone."

The doctor came back into the room with the nurse I was seriously beginning to resent following close behind. "Her heart is slowing down and she will soon be gone," he said, again lacking emotion. The nurse had a clipboard in her hand, and as soon as the doctor finished speaking, she asked if I wanted to donate my daughter's kidneys. Everything felt like a dream, a confusing dream—how could they be asking that? I believed she could live.

"No!" I snapped, "Her heart is still beating. Get in there and save her!" How could I give a kidney away? What if a miracle happened and she wasn't supposed to die? How would she feel waking without her kidneys? However, by some slim chance she didn't make it, I needed to be in the room with her when her spirit lifted from her body. She needed to see me there. I turned to the nurse to make sure she understood me correctly, "Leave her whole! Just leave her whole!"

I was eventually led back to Lanette's room but was told to wait at the door while they made sure her body was covered. I went in without waiting. Cover her body, I thought—from whom, her mother? I have seen her body, I gave birth to it. I have held it in my arms—I wasn't waiting, and time was precious. I reached for the sheet that covered her and removed it enough to hold her hand, and then I gently moved it again to run my hands over her legs. I touched a large bruised bump on her ankle—I knew it was broken. How I wished I had the power to make the injury go away. My hands ran over her feet. I smiled at her toenails—they were red—I nodded my head—that little monkey, she did use my nail polish. The smile quickly faded as I winced at how injured she was. Only twelve years old, that was too young to die.

The doctor came in and stood next to me. I stated in a supplicating voice, "She really is beautiful, you know? She doesn't look like it now, but she is, you know." It was as if I was trying to convince him how valuable she was, so he would work harder to save her. I felt he was giving up.

"I know," he answered, "accidents will do that."

As I left her room for the last time, I found myself looking over the faces of all the nurses to see if they realized what a tragic loss just took place. If they knew her like I did, they would be crying or they would be consoling me. They were all going about their business as usual, and no one bothered to cast a glance in the direction of a crushed woman whose life was draining out of her just as sure as the life of the young girl on the gurney was departing. How could they not spare a tear for a child whose future had just been snuffed out like a flame on a match or a tear for her empty chair at the table or the void her family would feel without her?

Gayle took my arm and said it was time for us to go. "You need to get home and let your husband know what has happened. Kathy, there is nothing more you can do."

"How can I just leave her here?" I asked. I had a million concerns. How will they treat her body? Where will she go when she leaves the room? Will they handle her with tenderness? Will they understand how precious her body is? After all, it housed her spirit for twelve years.

"Kathy," Gayle repeated, "let's go." She took my arm and led me toward the elevator. I slowly stepped in and turned to view the nurses' station one last time before I left. Before the doors closed, my eyes landed on a small gray-haired nurse, and running down her cheek, I spotted a tear. I locked eyes with her as she slowly wiped it away. The action and the tear pierced my heart. It was a tear that screamed every emotion I had been feeling. It was a tear for Lanette, and it meant someone understood. For the rest of my life, I will think of that tear and treasure it because I thought my daughter deserved at least one from someone who realized the sorrow in the loss of a child.

When someone has to place their loved ones into the hands of others, it would be nice to know that their last breath is taken in the presence of someone who still has a tear or two left in them, someone who is still vulnerable enough to share your pain, even for a moment. Now the tears will be mine and I will need to find the courage to live with them.

> Courage is not the towering oak that sees storms come and go;
> it is the fragile blossom that opens in the snow.
> — Alice Mackenzie Swaim

It takes a lot of courage to not only pursue the truth of your life, but to be in accord with it, recognizing what is, what has been, and what is yet to be. The nourishment of the soul is truth. Truth is acting in harmony with what is right and then having the courage to do something about it. Many will tell you that truth is elusive and sometimes impossible to discover, and that is why it is so often referred to as hidden, but it is not hidden. Yet truth is what you need to heal. There are different ways to becoming acquainted with truth, but two of the main ones are through your own experiences and by observing truth in the lives of others and pondering with a sincere heart and rightful intent for the witness of it. It is the hope of every sincere and loving soul to be conscious; that means to be aware of and in harmony with the spirit of truth. Desire the truth in your life and have the courage to search for it. It will take courage to read the following pages with an open heart, sincerely seeking for the light of truth to help you travel perhaps one of the most difficult journeys of your life. This is only a partial map because you must chart out the rest so you may connect again with the main highway without having to fall off every cliff and navigate every dangerous narrow road. Remember, there are many kinds of mountains: there is the kind my sister had to navigate over and the inner kind that calls to our souls to climb and find the peak that will heal us. By ignoring the mountain and turning from your courage, you will miss out on the opportunities of discovery. You can find it, but the ultimate work and the actual journey of your life will be on the roads that you choose to travel or the ones you blaze yourself, many times way beyond the beaten path.

Courage is not about strong fearless men or about the hero who risks his life in a flashing moment of danger as much as it is about every person having the courage to discover their personal victories. There are no boundaries, no criterion, or no demands that state what genuine courage is. There are those courageous acts that unacknowledged die with some but leave a legacy of virtue and decency behind, and then there are heroes who die forever unknown to man. There are those quiet acts of courage that are displayed when someone reaches out in their own pain to help someone else. There are those courageous people who stand for their belief even though no one is looking and those who pray even when they are ridiculed. Having the faith to be still, to ask for help, or to admit weakness takes courage. Thank God we all have the seed of courage that waits for the light to help it grow. Ordinary people can be the most exceptional messengers of courage because when they dare to be courageous, they are no longer ordinary.

> *Men wonder at the height of mountains, the huge waves of the sea, the broad flow of rivers, and the course of the stars—and forget to wonder at themselves.*
> *—St. Augustine*

If you want to shine like a diamond
In a world of rhinestones,
Allow the wisdom of light,
Blossoms of time
And winds of life,
To refine your heart
From a piece of glass
Into a valuable gem.

Seek

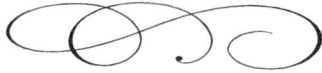

I heard a story about a woman who decided at a rather short notice that she wanted to see a Broadway play, so knowing her chances of getting a good seat might be difficult, she made up her mind that she would do whatever it took to obtain the best seat in the house. She bought the ticket and asked the box-office man if he considered it one of the best.

"Madam," said the box-office man, "it is a good seat, it is near the stage."

"Are you positive?" she asked two or three times.

"Madam," he answered impatiently, "if it was much closer, you would have to be in the play!"

It was late in the day, I was ready to close the office when the phone rang and I answered to hear an angry voice on the other end. It was an elderly woman informing me that she had received a bill from us and she wasn't going to pay it. She said we could try and squeeze it out of her, but she was never going to pay it. The anger in her voice wasn't unfamiliar to me; in fact, with each billing cycle, I came to expect a certain percentage of those types of calls. I always tried to handle them by allowing them to vent.

Her adult son had died and now of all things to have to deal with, a bill for his body to be transported to the medical examiner's facility. "No," she repeated, "I am not going to pay. Let the county pay for it."

I listened as I heard her voice start to crack. I knew she was trying to hold back tears. "You just don't know," she cried, "what this has done to my life. My pain is impossible to bear. Now I have to take care of my grandchildren and I don't know how I am going to do that. I have no money. I can't even force myself to get out of bed in the morning. Haul me away to jail, see if I care!" This was usually where the conversation shifted because it was always assumed that I couldn't possibly know what kind of pain each one was experiencing, but the truth was, I did know.

"I understand," I answered when a window of silence opened up the chance to speak. "I have been where you are, and I know it is inconceivable how a human can suffer like this and still live." I paused for a moment before I gently continued to speak. "You never know how strong you are until you have to hold on. You can hold on for your grandchildren, they need you now more than ever. They lost their daddy, who better to teach them to cherish his memory than you? I can assure you that someday you will be able to smile again, but now, the first thing you have to do is what I had to do: you have to hold on and begin to save your own life."

The string of events that landed me in that office seemed like an enigma. For twelve years, I owned a company that serviced funeral homes and the state and county medical examiner's offices, doing transports and various courier services. In the beginning, I started it with a partner who was a funeral director and a reconstructive art surgeon, and because it was his dream to start his own business in that field, he asked me if I would help him launch it. I agreed and decided to participate for the experience and the learning. Of all the career choices I could have chosen, this was never on a list of possibilities; in fact, it would have been on the list of types to avoid. Not many people desire to work among the dead. Yet I couldn't say no.

At the time, I was contently working in the music business, and it was definitely a more upbeat job, yet the timing and circumstances that plopped me smack dab into the heart of a business that dealt with death and grieving was not a random accident; it appeared because of a once-voiced plea to understand. When my daughter died, there had not been a question unasked about the industry that I found myself in need of even though I knew nothing about it. The questions never let up until I started working in the business.

When I first started, I carried a pager and spent many hours in the field, helping move and transport the deceased. I went to homes, hospitals, highways, and many other locations where people took their last breath of life. Many times, we were the first people the families had to deal with after a death occurred and our job was to console and assure them that their loved ones were in good hands. I learned to assist in prep rooms to prepare for viewings and stood in many times as county or state pathologists conducted autopsies to determine cause of death. I assisted like a nurse while someone's face was sewn back together after a terrible accident. I pulled little children out of cars, still clutching small toys in their hands, picked up stuffed animals, little dolls, or blankets as they lay strewn across the highway—always fighting back tears as I did.

I embraced babies as their mothers laid them in my arms to take to the funeral home. I observed the aftermath of murders, suicides, domestic abuse, and drug overdoses. I witnessed firsthand how many sorrowful things happen every day to so many people. Contrary to what I believed at first, the job helped me see that I was not alone and I had never been singled out. It didn't take me long to grasp the magnitude of a once humble plea on my part to understand, and there I was, with not only a glimpse of it, but a front-row seat.

After learning the ropes of the business, my partner pulled up stakes and left me with the company. I wasn't sure I could handle it alone, but I knew I had to. I had to stay and continue to connect the dots to understand how I could best serve people in their darkest hours. My first decision was to move into the office, turn the field work over to physically stronger people, and teach them to understand how important it was to be caring and compassionate. I still find it amazing how I asked to know a little and I received so much more. There I was on the other end of the line when grieving people called about one thing—and they got me.

It isn't easy to look back on life and try to capsulize so many events and so many learning experiences because each one either big or small got me where I am today. All my choices weren't the best, and I am not always sure they were placed before me to teach me or I placed them in my life because of my free agency, but I do know that in spite of everything, I became a better person.

In 1982, my mother was on chemotherapy for breast cancer. That year, she came to Arizona to spend a week with me over the spring break. I was worried about her, but she kept assuring me she was going to be all right.

One evening as I was doing the dinner dishes, she sat and read me an article from one of the local papers about a young man who had been working with weights and fell backward, hit his head—and bam, he was dead. I stared out the window as she read and a wave of fear swept through me. "What a terrible thing to happen," I remarked. "I can't imagine what his family must be going through." I quickly put the thought out of my mind because it hurt to think about. I convinced myself that God wouldn't expect me to survive something like that because he knew I wasn't strong enough. But that just wasn't so.

September approached, school started, and the hot lazy days of an Arizona summer were phasing out. Then my daughter died. Life changed—part of me died and grief threw me into a dark and scary abyss of fear, anger, and sorrow. Survival seemed impossible. A year later, I gave birth to a little girl, but she couldn't leave the hospital until they could determine what was causing her blood to be abnormal. I was afraid to get too attached to her because I knew I couldn't handle another loss.

My mother came to help with the house and the kids while I recuperated, then she went home to finish the last part of her journey on this earth. My sweet little baby girl came home and my mother went home to die.

My mother had been my emotional rock after Lanette died, and I couldn't fathom why God allowed my source of strength to leave me alone in my grief.

I read somewhere that some people who were very close to their spouses when they died usually followed within a matter of weeks or months. My father sank into great despair with my mother's death, and I didn't think he should be alone, so I offered him a home with my family. I watched in sadness as he suffered. I look back at that period, and it reminds me of someone who couldn't swim jumping in to save someone who was drowning. I couldn't swim, and my father was drowning. I would lie in bed at night and selfishly wish God would just stop my heart. It just didn't make sense; I still had three beautiful children who needed me more than ever and I wanted to die.

After burying my mother, I found out I was pregnant with my fifth child and carried it to term, and before delivery, it died. After I lost the baby, it seemed that life knocked me down over and over again. As is sometimes common when a death in the family happens, marriages begin to fall apart, and mine was no exception. By then, my health was declining and my son, Bryan, was always sick. The doctor informed us he had a compromised immune system when we almost lost him to chickenpox. With everything that kept happening, I became emotionally exhausted and suffered a mental breakdown. Throughout the following months, it felt like I was paddling a boat going nowhere, and it was everything I could do to function on a day-to-day basis.

The following summer, my family took a much needed vacation. We visited friends in Idaho. We rode horses, shared memories, and talked about life. We made plans to go out one evening to a lodge outside of town. The babysitter had been arranged and we were ready to leave when Bryan slipped on wet concrete in their garage. He fell asleep, and I couldn't wake him. We rushed him to the hospital, and by the time we arrived, he was unconscious. He had suffered a severe concussion, much like the one that had taken his sister's life only four years earlier. I sat vigil by his bedside for four days while he lay in a deep sleep, and I pleaded with God to spare his life.

Journal:

I was in a trance staring at all the wires attached to my poor little boy's head when the doctor came in and informed me that they were transferring him by ambulance to another hospital where they could conduct more tests on his brain. Depending on the outcome of the tests, they were standing by to fly him to the Salt Lake City Children's Hospital. I was more assertive this time and insisted on staying with him from the minute I brought him in and throughout the course of the whole ordeal. They wanted me to wait in another small room, but I refused and politely but firmly informed them that I would not be leaving his side. When they took him in to do a CT scan, I insisted on going in with him. They weren't happy about it, but allowed me to do it anyway. I stood next to him, holding his little hand while the technician strapped his head to the table. She pointed to a small window and said she would be in the next room getting the equipment setup and it would only take a minute. Several minutes had passed before I began to wonder what was taking her so long. Without moving away from the table, I tried standing on my toes to see if I could see her through the window, but I couldn't see anyone in the small room and about the time I realized no one could see us either, Bryan started to vomit. I grabbed the strap off his head and quickly turned him over so he wouldn't choke, and brutally realized had I not been standing there, he could have suffocated before they even knew what happened. My experience in the hospital with Lanette had given me the courage to insist that I be able to be near him at all times, which probably saved his life. When the ambulance arrived, I was given permission to ride in the back with him. I took his tiny hand in mine and was prepared to bargain with God. I thought about his sister and how I didn't get a chance to plead for her life before she died. How could this be happening again? I felt despair rising in me, and just as I was about to let it take over, I felt a warm rush of energy penetrate my whole being. I felt calm, and a small whisper assured me that my precious little boy was going to be all right. I felt the presence of his sister in the back of the ambulance with us, and I settled into a state of peace.

By the time the doctors had seen him and more tests were conducted, I was still embraced by the peace. It didn't matter if the doctor had grim news because I had an unexplainable knowledge that my son would be okay.

The doctor looked at me and said. "We were ready to put him on a flight to Salt Lake City, but his condition has dramatically improved and I actually think a couple more days of observation is all we will need and he should be ready to go home."

We arrived home grateful to have our little boy with us and embarking on a journey to help him deal with the injury to his brain. He would, through the course of his life, suffer flare-ups that affected his speech and balance. It was a speed bump in his life that would make some simple things hard to cope with and difficult things next to impossible, but he was alive and we had him.

When I started to get back on my feet, I visited my doctor, and standing with my chart in his hand, he told me he had failed to mention that the mammogram I had six months earlier revealed a lump in my left breast. What next? I thought, with feelings of panic starting to consume me. How in the world was I going to deal with that news?

More moves, the loss of jobs, and children battling their own demons of drug and alcohol use, a divorce, another failed marriage that ended with physical and emotional abuse and infidelity kept me paddling and paddling to stay afloat.

The first time I took my grandson Ayden to the pumpkin patch, he was about three. He was fearless when confronting the big corn maze. He watched as other children were running in by themselves, and he wanted me to let go of his hand. I was afraid to let him out of my sight, so I negotiated with him. I'd go first and stay just a little ahead of him, and if he felt lost, he could call me and I would be close enough to rescue him. I would not leave the maze until we were both safely out.

When he was seven, I joined him on a field trip with his school to another pumpkin patch with a much larger maze. There were a hundred screaming kids trying to enter at once, but Ayden wasn't quite sure if he could brave it alone.

"Go with me," he begged. "I'm afraid I'll get lost."

I was about to tell him to stay with the other kids, he'd be fine, but I encouraged him to take it slow, and if he came to a path he wasn't sure of, to stop and think for a minute because if he was heading in the right direction, he would eventually make it out.

"Go in before me," he pleaded again. "What if I never come out?"

"I'll stand on the outside," I told him, "If you feel lost, call out and I will hear you and you can follow my voice to the exit. If you have too though, you can head straight out to the sound of my voice right through the corn even if a path hasn't been hacked out. You will be on the outside of the maze in a hurry. Remember," I went on, "the real fun is in not giving up until you figure it out."

A Legitimate Journey

As history will show, he took off, made it out in a flash, and went back in for the second time. But what school do we attend to learn how to cope with loss or to help us navigate through the mazes of personal dilemmas, disappointments, and tragedies? Where do we find the strength and understanding to let us know we are not alone? Who can teach us how to listen, ponder, and hear the voice of someone who cares to lead us? If we could hover above the maze like angels, maybe it wouldn't be so difficult to view and navigate our way out.

There was a time I believed that I attracted pain and sorrowful events like a magnet attracts a million shards of metal. I looked back at the maze and wish I had taken different paths. Hindsight was always translucent. I would look at others and wonder why they were sailing right past all the jagged boulders and dangerous cliffs without so much as a scrape or a bump. Life certainly was appearing unfair. Yet moment by moment, I began to realize that unlike the lady who wanted a seat close to the stage, I would not have been content to be in the audience, I had to be in the play.

My play was a lifetime of experiences, many wonderful, many painful, and yet the curtain calls became wake-up moments, powerful lessons, and miracles, all of which delivered me here to the writing of this book. The ancient philosopher Epictetus once said: "No great thing is created suddenly, any more than a bunch of grapes or a fig. If you tell me that you desire a fig. I answer you that there must be time. Let it first blossom, then bear fruit, then ripen."

It's amazing the magic that time holds. We aren't as receptive to powerful life lessons and our own mortality as perhaps we are when life has given us age, painful experiences, and humility to awaken our senses to hearing heaven's voice try to help us through the maze. If I compared my life to a tapestry with the weaving never ceasing until my time on earth was up, then I have definitely come to see that the weaving is the living of my life, and at times, the cloth was rough and loose, but time has helped me see the fine golden threads woven in along the way—the threads of light, learning, and wisdom, which makes the tapestry a magnificent work of art. I clearly came to know that I did not want the sorrows in my tapestry to define me as much as I wanted it to reveal that I survived the sorrows to see the miracles so profoundly woven in. Like the philosopher told us, I had to blossom and then ripen. Truly, angels are hovering above the maze and they know the bigger picture. As I learned, it is wise to let them share their view once in a while.

If a path leads us to sorrow and we don't know where to turn, where do we look for a roadmap? It may seem impossible to find ourselves in the midst of pain, but through my scraped knees, my bumped head, and my injured heart, that is exactly where I found myself. When I started seeking and then asking, I started healing; when I started healing, I started seeing. I saw that all along, I was being taught how to get through to my encore. When I paid attention, teachers appeared and the road signs became obvious. If you are in pain and are suffering and don't know what to do, reach out, don't be afraid because miracles wait around every corner and you deserve to see them…start seeking the light.

Grief came today
While I was looking the other way.
It came with such fury and surprise.
It was unfamiliar to my eyes.
"Don't Stay!" I wailed,
"Please go away,
I don't have time for you today."
I felt its breath, but it lingered still.
"I cannot leave…It is not your will.
The time will come when I shall go,
But not until you come to know;
I am your friend and what I give,
Is understanding so you may live."

Grief

What comes to mind when you hear the word grief? For most people, grief depicts suffering or sorrow, pain beyond relief, or a period of mourning. Universally grief can be caused by many things like the death of a loved one, the loss of a relationship, a change in your life that is difficult to adjust to, or an illness. Webster's definition of grief is: a deep and poignant distress caused by or as if by bereavement.

Webster's term of bereavement is probably referring to experiencing the death of a loved one, but the truth is, grief can appear in someone's life for a number of reasons and at any time. It is an emotional, physical, and spiritual response to loss, and we have come to identify it as the process we go through to heal loss that is created from all kinds of life-altering events.

Grief is the emotional involvement of all our senses in direct proportion to whatever has come about in our lives that involves a sudden change or a loss that leaves us feeling powerless, sad, fearful or lonely. Grief can also come about because of the sorrow of regret that can be responsible for the downward spiraling emotions one feels when he believes he has hit rock bottom after a life of bad choices. This can be a self-imposed grief, but real nonetheless. The fact is, there are no set of rules that ordain grief or the kind of healing that can result as a product of it.

Situations can arise for a number of reasons that can plunge even the most valiant and strong people into a total and unwelcome state of suffering. Being prepared to receive grief is not usually a choice one decides to make, in fact, it is quite the opposite and most of us are totally unprepared because it is not something we wake up one morning and choose to prepare for.

A Legitimate Journey

It is healthy human nature to avoid dwelling too much on things we fear could knock our feet out from under us. Most of us don't stockpile a reserve of coping skills to help us get through a tragedy or traumatic event just in case one happens. Most people don't own a grief first aid kit capable of sparing their faith, saving their relationships, or saving their life. So when we hear of other's tragic losses, it is not unusual to push the thought out of our minds as quickly as possible, especially if it causes us pain. It's easier to assume those things only happen to other people until we realize we have become a member of "the other people" club, the ones that believed God knew they couldn't handle it.

There is a high probability that to experience life there will be painful events, possibly ones that could knock us off our feet or take the wind out of our sails, but they don't have to destroy us. Many good people have known adversity, great suffering, and loss but have found their way out of its grip and risen to a new level of compassion and gentleness. Growth from such events can come in unexpected ways. When sorrow strikes, it really isn't protection from feeling we need as much as it is the courage to face it and survive. If we choose to live this life and we choose to love, we can choose to ask for courage to let grief teach us.

Chances are if you are reading this book, you have probably suffered a loss or know of someone close to you that has. Maybe you are faced with a traumatic event in your life that has knocked the wind out of you. Maybe you are ill and desire to know how to feel peace or help your loved ones help you. If you try to count the reasons, you will find they are endless.

People used to struggle to find the right words to say to me—words that could comfort me or help me forget my pain, but there are no words that possess instant magic, but I bless them for trying, they meant well. What I needed was the faith to believe that I could smile again and the energy to do the work to get there.

An emotional wound profound enough to cause grief is very much like an open physical wound that needs to heal, except that the healing of the emotions is finding closure in your inner world of thoughts. When the spirit cannot heal, it can affect the physical body in many ways. Grief is what has to take place for healing to begin...it really is a matter of survival. To avoid this process and try to wish it away can lead to adverse effects both physically and spiritually. Hanging on to pain too long can negatively impact every cell of our bodies. When an infected spirit moves into physical illness because of unresolved grief, it can literally rob you of your life.

I had experienced different depths of grief prior to Lanette's death, but none that had catapulted me into a state beyond pain and I couldn't comprehend how a human was supposed to live through it. I awoke that Friday morning, the sun was shining and a wonderful breeze was dancing through the willow tree in the front yard, but by evening, my life as I knew it, was no more. I was numb, shocked, and unable to gather even the slightest activity of thoughts. The blessed numbness got me through the funeral, but when it wore off, I was left with an overwhelming despair. All I could think of was how I wanted to die and go be with her.

Journal:

Lanette died...the funeral came and went in a dream like haze. All the people that showed up with casseroles, meals, desserts, and cards were gone. A new week had been ushered in the day my mother left to go home. I stood on the driveway as I tearfully hugged her good-bye. She got in the car, closed the door, and waved. I saw her sobbing as the car pulled away. I turned and my eyes settled on the leaves of our willow tree, again gently waving in the breeze, then my eyes slowly swept over all the other trees on the street, waving back and forth as if in synchronized rhythm. The breeze that had been so welcomed before was now painful to watch. I sat down on the grass under the tree; I cried and couldn't believe that God was allowing the world to just keep moving on as if nothing had happened.

The death of a loved one is likely the toughest form of grief to work through, especially if it is sudden and there was no time to say good-bye— perhaps because death seems so final and can't be undone, but I will never diminish other causes of grief because it would disregard individual suffering that can take place for many reasons and the severity of its effects. Simply put, pain is pain and it is unique to everyone.

The depth of grief is proportionate to the extent of which we have loved or lived. Divorce may manifest many of the same challenges as a death because it manifests similar symptoms of anguish such as separation, loneliness, change in habits, and feelings of betrayal, which some people feel as well when a loved one has died. Grief is a very personal thing to experience, and yet it can also be universal because it is our human capacity to love that makes us aware that grief transcends all barriers of race, religion, or ethnicity.

Everyone's expression of grief can be as different as night and day; however, as different as it may be, surrendering to it does not mean that we are giving up our hope for a continuation of life or in regaining the same quality of it we had before. Our grief is proof that our love was real and that our need to find closure is because we know in the deepest part of our reality that like it or not, we must go on and have the courage to find our place in a changing season of our own existence.

One great lesson I learned was that there was nothing like a crisis to test a person's inner strength and pioneer him to a deeper understanding of who he is. Once a person starts to question his life, his purpose, and his priorities, his senses begin to change and a new life starts to form.

After Lanette's death, for the first time I could ever remember, I felt powerless. My destiny, it seemed, was no longer in my hands; for where I once thought I was the captain of my ship, I was suddenly being tossed about in a raging sea with no compass or navigational tools to see me to shore. I believed I wasn't strong enough to navigate the raging sea of my life. Where was the lighthouse?

It is not unusual for people who have lost a loved one to go through this process. I was certainly trying to find explanations for "why me," but there were none.

If grief is truly the emotional and spiritual response to loss, then it should be the teacher that brings us to an enlightened healing, one that renews and restores us to hope in living. It is very seldom that someone comes to this earth and escapes it totally. If you begin to understand this, then you can begin your journey to healing. The saying that there must be opposition in all things is true, especially if it applies to life. You cannot know light if you do not know darkness. You cannot know joy if you have never known sorrow. When you find peace again, it will be sweeter than you ever remembered. People who have weathered the storm will tell you that some of their greatest lessons have come from some of their most trying experiences.

How is it that some people live most of their life and escape life changing grief? I don't know, but most don't. I remember reading about George Wald, a Nobel Prize winner, who said at sixty-nine that he had never seen a person die or even been in the same house where death occurred. It wasn't until he was sixty-eight that an obstetrician friend invited him to witness a birth. He wondered himself how some of life's greatest events have been willfully taken out of our experience. How is it we hope to live full emotional lives when we purposely try to protect ourselves from some of life's deepest human emotions? He went on to say that with no experience of pain, how are we expected to understand joy?

The unwelcomed grief that started me on my journey through heartbreak led me to a life of light and understanding. It is this kind of light I want to share. We don't have to suffer to understand it, but sadly, it is most often sorrow that propels us into seeking answers that can help us cope with the pain. We are more likely to seek when our heart is broken. I was no different.

There are numerous books about grief and many of them are very helpful. Research has shown that the stages of grief are very similar among most people. They acknowledge that "grief work" is necessary to accomplish a healthy healing, yet with each case, there is an element of individuality that must keep us from putting everyone in the same category, time wise and emotionally. Although counseling and therapy can help us grieve, there is no exact method. We can't hurry people along or dictate how they should deal with any one of the stages.

The first stage is the merciful stage of numbness and shock. During this time, one moves like a robot in order to get through taking care of arrangements and making timely decisions. This protects the body from a complete shutdown. After the numbness wears off, sorrow sets in, and with sorrow comes the fear of loneliness, and after a certain amount of time, anger will usually show its unproductive head—unproductive because the negative emotion can slow down healing. Until the anger passes, one can be at a standstill. After anger has mellowed, hope can arrive, and with hope, surrender. Surrender does not mean you agree with what has happened, but it helps you realize that you can't change it or rewind time, and all the "what ifs," "if only," and "why me" slowly start moving to the back of your mind so healing thoughts can move you into the present.

Grief work is about finishing unfinished business. Grieving is suffering, but it is legitimate suffering, and until we begin the legitimate journey of moving forward, we cannot move past it. Of all the times in our lives when we need to take the first steps of a journey, it is during grief.

I have shared with you what research has shown and other authors have written about grief. Perhaps it is an academic or clinical approach to understanding the different stages, and it helps to know some of these things so that we can feel we are normal, that is, as normal as can be and by whose definition, but when we are moving into our own uncharted territory, we want to know we are not the only one who has experienced these things. That's why support groups have proven to be a great resource because it lets us know we are not alone.

Suppose I told you that you don't have to suffer endlessly, and while you are right in the middle of your grief, you could live, love, and even laugh. The earth and all the universe is alive with awareness and enlightenment and we are on the crest of a new day where skeptics can't even argue about heaven opening its windows to show us a glimpse of it. Suppose you could witness miracles and see the impossible? What if you could know that we are more than our physical bodies and every step we take toward learning and love will open a window to see a place beyond this world?

I can't explain why you are suffering and others are not, but it is my hope that I can lead you to the tools to help you live through it. If you are tired of talking and listening to the nudging of others to get better and move on, then perhaps it is time to let go of that which isn't working and look for another way to experience growth. Every person who has traveled through their grief and found the magic of joy again had to surrender their will to change the old habits that left them treading water. There is a way to the truth of healing and it is into the light. Go on this journey with me into the light. I ask that you crumble any walls that skeptically surround you and set doubt aside for the duration of these pages. If you do, your view will change so your healing can begin. Making it through grief isn't just a matter of stopping the pain, but in making your life joyful and fulfilling again.

There is a room with a window to your right
And if your heart is ready,
You may catch a glimpse of light.
Just a glimpse or a passing view,
Maybe not much more,
But when God gives you a window,
He usually gives a door.
Does it hold the answers
You've searched for, oh so long?
Perhaps a love or a melody
That fills your heart with song.
If the light cannot stop you
Long enough to ask for more,
What friend, what life,
What miracle do you leave behind the door?

The Light

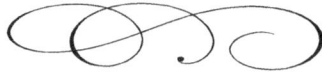

Visualize, if you will, that you are standing outside the door of a large room that sets inside a beautiful modern building. You came to this building because a friend encouraged you to. This friend wanted you to find the desires of your heart. He was a trusted friend, and for that reason, you did not hesitate to come. Passionately, this friend tells you that beyond that beautiful ornate door is a majestic room, and in that room is a multitude of dimensions that have answers to questions you have hungered for all your life.

You stop to think for a minute and then ask yourself what questions those could be. You turn and ask your friend how he came to know of this room when you have never heard of it. So, as is your nature, you start to doubt the truth of his revelation. Still, your friend encourages you to just open the door and walk in. He assures you that you will not be disappointed. So you place your hand on the large golden knob but do not turn it because you notice that your hand is trembling. Perhaps, you wonder, you're nervous about what you may actually find in there. You think for another second, only to question who could possibly know the desires of your heart, and if they were staring you in the face, would you recognize them?

You think about your life and some of the turbulent waters you've had to sail. You think about unfulfilled dreams, heartbreaks, and disappointments. What would you ask for if a genie could grant you three wishes? Hmmm…you just stare at the door and think for a moment.

Before long, your curiosity has the best of you. What choice do you have but to just turn the knob and enter the room? You will never hear the end of it if you don't. Even if there is nothing in there and your heart's desires are not revealed, what have you lost? However, what if you discover things you don't want to know? You now start to second-guess yourself again , maybe you think you could just turn and walk away and never know what you would be missing, and quite frankly, not knowing what you didn't know wouldn't hurt you...would it?

However, you go ahead and turn the knob. Before you step into the room, you turn to your friend and ask, "Are you certain that the desires of my heart will be manifested?"

"I told you so, didn't I?" came a soft answer. "One glance at the contents of the room and you will recall dreams, hopes, and see new things that had you known about them before, you would have pursued them with all your heart. You just need to enter, and you will understand."

A gentle unspoken whisper nudges you to go forward. "What have I got to lose?" You laugh skeptically and step onto the threshold. If you owned any sense of adventure and courage before, it disappeared when you stood there trying to peer into a room so dark that even the brightest sun could not penetrate the blanket of blackness. You stop and refuse to go in because, no one knows this, you are afraid of the dark. Not only do you convince yourself that it is much too dark for you, but you're sure there could actually be something unsafe in there. Fear of the unknown is what you tell yourself is going to keep you from going in. "Is this a joke?" you ask.

Now imagine a couple of scenarios. You can make a choice, and let's imagine that one is you irritably turn away from the room, maybe even slam the door, and walk away, going so far as to grumble about this being a waste of your time. Just like you questioned before, did you really miss what you never knew?

Now, let's imagine another choice. You are standing at the entrance to the same room. You are told the same thing about what is in the room, but this time you agreed to go because you needed something, but you are not sure what. Your friend knew this and led you to the door. You were grateful for his caring and you are hoping that your search might be fruitful.

Again, you are told that all you have to do is turn the knob and enter the room. You don't hesitate, even though you are not sure what you are looking for, only that you are longing for something, and because you know that if you can't find it there, you will have to keep searching. Hoping you will find something, and believing that it was no accident that you were led here, you turn the knob.

You are standing at the threshold and you behold a dark room in front of you, but you do not turn away because you remember you were told you must enter the room. You enter and tell yourself that maybe understanding is something you feel more than you see. You tell yourself that this is possible. A whisper tells you to enter, leave your fears behind, and reach out. With your arms stretched out in front, you step in and start moving further into the room, and then you are inspired to ask if there is a light you can turn on.

You hear, "Take two more steps in. Lift your arms above your head and you will feel a chain…pull the chain."

You no sooner ask for the light and you are guided to its source. You pull the chain and everything in the room is illuminated to such a bright clarity that you can see everything in there. However, what you find so amazing is that you not only see what is in that room, but you can see beyond it into yet another and another until you realize that the rooms are never ending. Each one is connected to another and yet you see through the brilliant light what is in each one. You don't even feel the need to analyze the magnificent contents because somehow, the source of light has already done that for you. You stand there feeling like it is supernatural, but you can't deny that you have just moved into a new world of awareness, a world you did not know existed. You turn to your friend who is standing in the light with you and with such gratitude you have never felt before; you thank him for leading you to the door. You now understand what he meant when he said you will find everything you longed for and more. You weren't sure before what that everything was, but now you are—it was the light.

We all have a journey to find that room. For many, the journey doesn't even begin until a longing exists or our hearts need comfort or hope. Many a troubled heart has admitted that there was nothing more powerful than adversity to lead them to the light.

When you enter a room and flip on a light switch, you are using a tool, the lightbulb, as a means of seeing something that your eyes would not normally be able to see. However, because you walk into a dark room without the use of that lightbulb to illuminate the contents doesn't mean that the room is empty. Anyone that has ever tripped over a chair or a pair of shoes in a dark room will probably not disagree that because you can't see the contents, they are not there. They might even admit that being in the dark turned out to be quite painful. Yet typically, the human mind has a tendency to rationalize that which it can't see—doesn't exist.

When we create tools that enable us to see more clearly that which was essentially nonexistent becomes existent. Physical light, as we know it, is a frequency of energy. If you change the frequency, you change the light. Therefore, the higher the frequency, the more light…the more light, the more you see.

Before electricity, physical light used to be derived from either the sun or fire, and then someone with a believing mind was convinced that even though you couldn't see electricity, it existed. Because of this belief, a brighter form of light became a reality for everyone. Light in the spiritual sense represents the same kind of light. It is real and it represents energy. When we say we must bring something to understanding, we can also mean we must bring something to light. When we have a tendency to be confused, we may say we need to shed some light on the subject. When a person is at the height of his consciousness, we may say he is enlightened. The word light in any way that we use it represents pretty much the same thing, a frequency of energy or a frequency of awareness.

When I write about the light and bringing it into your life, I am not referring to the lightbulb or physical light as you know it, but a light nonetheless, which is still very much a part of the energy that the physical universe releases, which is critical to life on our planet. But just as physical light is necessary for physical life, so is nonphysical light essential to our nonphysical self. Your nonphysical self or your spirit is real energy. Nonphysical light is as real as physical light and it has energy vibrations just as the lower physical light does, yet it expands our souls to higher levels of awareness.

The Light

When you seek the higher light of the spirit, you become empowered with senses that go beyond your normal five physical senses. When you are able to tap into those other senses, you are considered to be a multi-sensory person. When you are authentically empowered with light so that your spiritual eyes can see, you have more ability to see and live in a higher state of awareness. This state of awareness is available to everyone. When you view light in your life as a source to understanding and compare light to truth and wisdom, you will see things that you did not know existed and you will understand truths that darkness would have kept you from seeing. Fear and darkness, the opposites of light, will be replaced with light, love, and understanding. Living in this kind of light will be like entering that proverbial dark room, now full of light with the increased ability to see everything that the spirit needs to see to become fully conscious, awake, and free from fear, worry, and hopelessness.

You have a higher nonphysical self that responds naturally to light, which is truth. When your spirit hears the truth, it recognizes it instantly. The spirit trusts wisdom and reacts to it spontaneously, whereas the physical mind insists on receiving scientific evidence. Just like the newly planted seed of a flower cannot grow to its intended beauty without the physical light the sun provides, so like the seed, our spirits cannot grow without the unseen spiritual light of truth and consciousness. Spirituality needs the fertile grounds of love, harmony, and inner awareness to grow.

Journal:

Sensing sadness from my youngest daughter, now an adult, I set aside my plans to try and help her through what was apparently another bout of depression. I didn't want to sermonize to her that she could turn it over to God because I know when darkness has taken over your life; you fight to believe such a simple solution. If it were that easy, we wouldn't have much need for psychotherapists, antidepressants, and mental hospitals. I talked about asking for help and allowing the light to come into her life so she could understand what way to turn. I shared stories with her about my own periods of sadness and depression and how I was sure I would never get through them. We talked for hours, and when night came, I put my arms around her and asked if she felt any better. She said she did, so we both retired for the night. I prayed that she could grasp the simple but profound concept of seeking the light, because I knew if she could, she would eventually discover her divine purpose.

I awoke the next morning, hoping that our talk the day before had given her some reprieve from her pain. I questioned what else I could have said to make my point. I talked with her about how many times miracles appear but we don't recognize them. I wanted her to know how humbling it is when you catch a glimpse of even the smallest one.

The summer before, I bought several small geraniums to fill the pots on our patio. I knew that the Oregon winters would be too hard on them. I considered them to be annuals and didn't expect them to survive, even though I couldn't resist clearing off a wooden workbench under a large window in the garage and moving them in under it. Maybe I could save them so they could come back in spring. During the busy winter activities, they always slipped my mind, but once in a while, I'd look over at them and give them a little water.

The morning after our talk, I stepped out into the garage and my attention was immediately directed toward the pots. It was late January and the nights had gotten pretty cold, yet the geraniums were thriving. They had large green leaves that looked healthy and shiny, yet every plant was pushing to one side of their pot and leaning into the window as if they were screaming, "We need the light!" My heart jumped and I looked up and said, "Thank you," and excitedly called my daughter to the garage. "I want to show you something," I said with excitement and directed her attention to the shelf. "Remember when I brought the geraniums in here hoping they would survive the winter? I didn't have much hope, but look! This is what I was trying to tell you. They have been struggling, fighting for their lives and look what they have done, they have turned to the light and they are flourishing. God's beautiful creations are wise enough to seek the light." It was one of those miracles.

The Light

Our minds need to surrender to our spirits to begin to flourish like the flowers. When we replace fear with light and love, we tap into our soul. When your spirit is illuminated, then you magically begin to see what others cannot and you begin to have a knowing that only you can know. The wonderful thing about this is: when you trust what your soul knows, no one will have the ability to silence you and you lose your need to prove anything to anyone.

You will have your own truths. You will have the ability to move through this life with everything you need, including, but not limited to, peace and understanding about life on this earth and life where our spirits reside because our spirits are eternal.

You will find yourself believing in miracles and you will be able to manifest miracles in your life, and the things people refer to as supernatural events will be normal to you because you will understand the laws of the universe and how they apply to everyone.

To understand this wonderful principle of light, you have to accept that your spirit was created perfectly. Knowing this helps you recognize your true empowerment. It will give you the power to receive a higher plane of understanding, potential, and truth. If you know this, you will have the ability to have true authorship over your life story. Your true self will rise above your mind's ability to bully you by telling you all the reasons why life is unfair and situations are hopeless.

If you will embrace the fact that you are a spiritual being and start with the most basic choice to choose love over fear, you will have the key to unlock the door and let the light in.

Your spirit and your soul is a conscious loving intelligence, created with perfection, and their purpose is to love and be loved. Embrace the truth that you are a spirit in a body who has a mind. You have a mind, but you are not your mind. This understanding is necessary for you to discover your soul and the light that feeds it. You and everyone around you, your loved ones, your neighbors, and people in other lands were all born for a reason. You are on this earth and you have a mission. Everything isn't just thrown here by accident with no plan or purpose. When you understand this, you must also understand that who we are does not cease when we leave our body and this earth.

When we embrace the term consciousness, we are embracing the fact that we exist. We know we exist! Consciousness is our intellectual soul essence and enables us to make successful choices by studying truth and learning from our experiences. Conscious intelligence is allowing our mind to be directed by our spirit and soul or putting it in more simple terms: letting in the light.

The purpose of this book is to help you see the light so you can see the contents of the room, which is your life here on earth. It is to help you understand the bigger picture so that you may feel peace, love, and have hope in all that you do so that you can live your calling.

Someone once told me that my grief had the ability to do two things and the choice was mine. It could make me a bitter, unhappy person or it could make me a more understanding, compassionate person. I wanted to be on the side of compassion. I hope you will open the door and see what I have brought back from my travels through grief. While on my journey over the mountains, the tough terrains, and the sorrowful valleys, I made a map to help others navigate their journey with fewer pitfalls. I am sure everyone that travels this road will see things I missed and be able to add to the map. Your entire journey will be just that—your journey, yet by contributing to the map, mankind can benefit from what you've learned.

Oliver Wendell Holmes wrote, "Man's mind, stretched to a new idea, never goes back to its original dimension."

The finish line of life isn't always in plain view, but the path is easier to see with light. As with any journey, it begins with the first step. Open the door and move in.

It is no mystery
No paradox of confusion or lack of light,
He feeds the soul the power to know
Which road to travel which way to go.
Some are blinded, hearts hardened
When rebuked by raging sea,
But fear not, he is the captain of your ship
His grace can steer you free.

God

there is a large billboard that sets beside the main freeway where I live that reads: "When you die, you will meet God. "Driving by it one day, I asked my daughter if she agreed with the sign.

"I don't know," she replied, looking at me a little perplexed. "I didn't even notice it, so I haven't given it much thought."

I suppose most people believe there is some kind of divine power operating in the world, just maybe not sure how it fits into their daily existence. If you were to ask people on the street to give you their impression or understanding of God, probably a large percentage of them would tell you they believe God to be someone dwelling in a remote place, maybe called heaven, and when we die, we will go there to meet him. Maybe we will be standing before him and he will flip the pages of his big book to see how many strikes we've managed to get against us while we regrettably or shamefully wait. In this day and age, however, few are satisfied with the limited understanding of this concept.

The subject of God may immediately construct a wall around some people; however, if you are going to walk through the door and into the light, it will require a faith in the existence of a Divine Creator. Refusal to believe we are part of a universal plan created by an intelligent and knowing creator will not change what is—you just won't be able to see clearly—much like that pair of shoes in a dark room. A simple seed of faith, a simple plea for understanding, and maybe a friend to lead you to the door will inspire you take the first step into a powerful world of awareness.

Everything that surrounds you and your life has a purpose and a plan. You may look around and observe people, ones who don't believe in God, yet they appear perfectly well without a care in the world, but no one has a clear view of what is going on in the inner world of others.

A Legitimate Journey

Journal:

Fall was swiftly moving along and all the bustling activities that fall brings was coming and going like it had done every fall before and I was still wondering why God hadn't stopped the world. My sister and her husband had tickets to go see an Arizona State football game and invited us to come along. I didn't want to go, but they wanted to get me out of the house and around people. They were worried about me—so I went. I sat in the bleachers high above rows of excited and happy people and the noise and festivities saddened me. My eyes scanned the crowd on the other side of the stadium and I winced at how many thousands of people were there on that night, and all of them whooping it up and having a good time. I asked myself why, out of the thousands there, I had to be the one to lose my child. I was deep into all the emotions of grief and finding it very difficult not to be angry. As I sat there, my eyes continued to scan over the crowd and they came to rest on a family three rows below us with a little boy who appeared to be about six or seven and his head had been shaven to reveal a large new scar that went from the top of his head to the back of his neck. Another scar went across the back of his head from one ear to the other. I sucked in a deep breath and wondered what terrible thing had happened to that poor child; my heart ached for the worry and fear his family probably had to suffer to save him. My heart began to soften. When my eyes made another sweep of the crowd, I saw something different. I realized everyone had a story, and who can say or know what it is? Maybe others were feeling the same thing I was, but we were there at the game, excitement all around, and our suffering was unknown to anyone but ourselves. Every life has their story.

When I visualize an image of God, I see a universally intelligent being that creates and inspires all life with love and intelligence so that we may experience life for all that it is meant to be. I knew him before I came here. I can know him while I walk upon the earth. I can have him with me, near me, and part of me. I do not have to die to meet him. I have already met him. I agreed to his plan before I came here, and by knowing his light, I can know of his love and have a fulfilling life. I see a Father, a parent like myself, who wants the best for his children. An image in my mind leads me to the room beyond the door, and I can see a figure, one that I am created in the likeness of, and on his face, I see many things. I see compassion, I see understanding, but most of all, I see wisdom. For all the mistakes that I berate myself for making, I do not see criticism and judgment on his face because in his wisdom, he knows that every one of those choices were a refining teacher. I see his arms outstretched, and somehow, I know that he wants to put them around me and say, "Do not fear." I grasp that he wants me to partake of the joys and blessings of love and abundance that he generously provides, but somehow, the light has pulled me in to understand that it does not come without the journey of my physical life. We don't meet him for the first time when we die, but we do need to reacquaint ourselves with him while we are on this earth so we may find the secret to a happy existence.

It may appear that some are blessed to know and understand their purpose and gifts of the spirit without tragic events, hurtful experiences, or wandering alone in the wilderness, but the key word here is appear because no one can really know what each person's life's journey has to teach them. Only our Creator knows, and each person's work toward spirituality is a private inner work. Skepticism abounds with reasons to substantiate the reasons why a God cannot exist, after all, there is no scientific proof, but when we no longer have the strength to keep arguing that God is not real, we usually find ourselves wishing he were. At one time or another, it is probable that everyone for whatever reason reaches an impasse that ends with a longing, a seeking, or a broken heart that only divine understanding can heal. It is no accident that this happens.

For many of you reading this, it will be like preaching to the choir; however, it is healing to reaffirm, but for others, a conviction of this fact has remained all too elusive until they find themselves in need of answers that will provide peace of mind and hope. I can say with assurance that knowing you are divinely created is taking the first step on the road that will lead you there.

How do I know these things? I believe I knew them before I came to earth, and by the grace of God, we all possess the light within us to know, but we have to pull the chain or turn on the switch. This source of divinity is beyond what we physical beings can truly understand unless we have the aide of our spiritual senses to enlighten us. Sometimes, we have to work to be aware of it. The work of consciousness and awareness takes discipline. It's actually miraculous when you come to know that all knowledge and wisdom are already programmed into that part of our unconscious selves that many of us don't even know exists. Our unconscious is wiser than we are about everything, and while it may appear to be a miraculous phenomenon to tap into, you can become aware of the treasure trove of wealth and wisdom that is there waiting for you.

It is by divine grace that we have been given the light that is available to us, not because we have earned it or because we are Bible scholars, but because we are loved. In whatever degree or manner it comes to us, it comes as a gift. It is that light that gives us the ability to recognize truth. If you read the scriptures and want to know in your heart what you read is true, it is that light that will witness to you what you need to know. This knowledge and truth is contained in our minds by grace, we inherited it from our Creator. However, part of the process of learning how tap into it is to seek it, to learn to be still long enough to let it teach us. It is not easy, but it is worth it.

For some, it might seem easier to believe that God does not exist because it relieves them of the responsibility and stewardship they have over their lives. That is why millions run away from the notion because believing in God places demands on them. Some fear that God may expect them to take upon ourselves impossible tasks and obligations they are not capable of. Besides, who wants to think all the time about what God actually wants from us? A lot of people just don't want to work that hard. As long as God is in heaven and we are here, we can let him have all the responsibility for mankind's evolution. For some, it's enough just to reach a comfortable old age, raise happy children, and peacefully coast until we die. Then, we can jump off the merry-go-round of life, and if there is a God, he can take over. It may also seem too difficult to put in the work that is required to nourish the spirit; however, like many other things, nothing of great value comes without the work required to understand it.

In spite of scientists, theologians, or self-proclaimed atheists, it is impossible to ignore that the universe was created in a glorious organized manner. God is logical, and he works within the realm of natural laws, and natural laws in and of themselves are very scientific.

Tapping into the gift of knowing this doesn't mean you have to immediately run out and find a church and start reading the Bible every day. You only need to have a desire to understand, then a seed of faith to ask.

We may all have different wishes how we want God to look or see where he resides, but within each person is a subconscious intellect that wants to know, and that knowing can speak many things to us. The inner world of who you are can be mirrored back when you see the one standing in that room beyond the door so full of compassion and wisdom. Jesus admonished us to seek the kingdom of heaven within, and he is referring to you, your inner mind, and your soul.

It used to be that scientists possessed a good case of tunnel vision, because if you couldn't see something, then it just didn't exist. M. Scott Peck, MD, says that even science is a religion because it is a world-view of considerable complexity. We know the universe is real, we know natural laws exist, thereby making certain things predictable. It would seem if God is logical that even he would operate within certain laws. It used to be if you couldn't measure something, a means by which scientists for centuries used to prove or disprove something, it just didn't exist, but in this day and age, the wonders of technology helps us measure things we never believed were measurable, let alone possible. Today's scientific-minded view of God has drastically improved, and maybe, someday, scientists will come to understand that both views are essential to the journey of spiritual growth. What we need to keep in mind is: that even scientists are human, and like most humans, we would rather have our answers easy to find and simple to understand.

Theologians and scientists have rarely been in agreement with each other, but that is changing because at least they are in agreement that because you can't see something with the human eye does not mean it does not exist. If scientists believed that, then the microscope would have never been invented nor would we understand the existence of atoms, electrons, subatomic particles, germs, viruses, and the DNA that makes up every personal blueprint. They are all forms of energy, and energy has no boundaries and no dimensions and it is not always visible to the eye, but it is real and it is this kind of energy that makes us who we are. Believing only what you can see is a lower plane of thinking, and as long as one clings to that, the higher stages of spirituality will remain a mystery.

When I hold a newborn in my arms, I can't help but marvel and think about what perfectly organized intelligence brought together such a magnificent and perfect creation, one that can grow to think, to reason, to love, and to create. My truth witnessed that people were not just an accident who figured out how to bring their cells together and then build a world to surround them.

The scientific principle of Ockham's razor is a scientific principle that states, "When two competing theories are being offered to describe the same system, the simplest most logical explanation is probably correct." Of course, that theory could generate a lot of arguments about being correct or perfect, but many thousands of applications have proven this to be correct most of the time. Yet in our DNA, the light of truth is built into each one of us so when we simply ask, we will be led to understanding.

Anyone can go on the Internet these days and research theories that will attempt to convince us there is no God, but you can also search all the data that says there is a one. Research can be stimulating and certainly give us much to think about, but without your inner truth meter, you cannot safely arrive at too many conclusions. It is the light within that will manifest your greatest knowledge. The scientific human mind will not be the avenue by which your enlightened high consciousness will be reached.

Sometimes, the reason the topic of God can weigh so heavily on the minds of unbelievers is because God is persistently pressing the issue of his existence all the time. A good example of that is given from the author C. S. Lewis who wrote about an unrelenting feeling to think about God every time his mind lifted from his work. He didn't desire to think about him or meet him, but he finally gave in and had to admit that God was God and, for the first time, knelt and prayed. He said he felt like the most dejected and reluctant convert in all of England. Lewis went on the write a book titled, *Surprised by Joy*; it was a result, he said, "of knowing God."2

Some people believe that the universe began with one enormous explosion of energy and light, often referred to as the big bang theory, but think about it, even that would have taken a source of intelligence to methodically line up every element to make it happen. The simplistic explanation has to be: only intelligence could do that.

If you personally want to know that God exists, he has said, "You will seek me and find me: when you seek me with all your heart, I will be found by you."

Seeking is not difficult, asking is easy, and neither requires a great sacrifice or price on your part. God is the author of our existence. He is the relationship that makes our existence meaningful. All the things in life that we crave, such as strength, joy, wisdom, and knowing we are loved, God gives as we listen and trust in him. He is our greatest reliable guide in life. Just as he engineered DNA to instruct the cell, he instructs us to make our lives function well.

What's comforting and amazing is that God does not force us to believe in him, but if you look, he does provide sufficient proof of his existence. You have to stop long enough to notice though. M. Scott Peck, MD, in his book *The Road Less Traveled* writes that most people need to have complete proof of God and miracles. We keep looking for the burning bush that Moses saw, and if we can't part the sea, then God has abandoned us. Then we ask, why doesn't God speak to us in a loud bellowing voice so that there can be no confusion of his existence? In today's world, our frame of reference is too dramatic. Not many want to stop long enough to look at our ordinary day-to-day events and notice the evidence of miracles all around us. It is just too simple. Yet it is possible to maintain a scientific slant at the same time miracles are happening around us, small and large, every day.

Dr. Peck's writings made a great contribution in the mental health industry, and through his efforts of helping to heal many lives, he came to the conclusion that there is a God and he can be present in all of our lives if we seek and ask for him.

A Legitimate Journey

As someone who has engaged in personal therapy, I was dismayed at how often the topic of God was not only avoided, but when I brought it up, it was usually skimmed over quickly, probably because the subject of God is perceived as religion and many religions are connected with control, but knowing God is about trusting our light of discernment. I had to understand that my personal relationship with God wasn't supposed to be molded by someone else's beliefs or non-belief's, even if they learned it from a psychology textbook, but in seeking and asking for my center of truth. If you want to understand God and see miracles in your life, stop, listen, and pay attention. When you begin to know God, you are tapping into the knowledge that your unconscious was already programmed with.

Scientists may say this concept is too basic, yet how can God be so intimately associated with us and a part of us if this is not so? If we are told to seek the kingdom of heaven within, then it is within us to know. If we desire to find wisdom greater than our own, God has placed it inside of us. Dr. Peck suggests that we try to understand that the interface between God and man is somewhat in part the interface between our unconscious and our conscious. So think about looking within and understand God is very much a part of us, he is now, and always has been.

Extraordinary phenomena can seem commonplace if you just pay close enough attention to it. Miracles that surround us all the time are taken for granted. If you open your heart and seek the truth, how do you suppose you will recognize it? The word recognizes means to re-know, so if you knew it once, where did it come from?

Before I formed thee in the belly I knew thee; and before thou camest forth out of the womb I sanctified thee.
Jeremiah 1:5

Knowing God isn't about being afraid or having the energy to sacrifice our lives or having to do such hard work that we become exhausted. It isn't about having to step in and attempt to run everyone else's life either. Knowing God is about tapping into the peace, the comfort, and the wisdom that can actually bring us wellness. It's about looking beyond the one room and seeing all the things we didn't know about the other room. It's about standing in awe of how great and powerful we are and about how loved and valued we are. Knowing God should never give us reason to fear, but reason to be happy. We are all created with that inner light of consciousness, and when we tap into it, we become aware of all that our Creator has made available to us. There is wisdom in the fact that we must seek him. He doesn't want to force us. Our unconscious is packed with knowledge beyond our mortal ability to grasp, but when we enter the room and ask for the light, we transcend beyond the mortal understanding of things. It is God who is the source of all that is. He is the beginning and the end, the Alpha and the Omega. Open the door, "pull the chain," and believe in him.

"There are two ways to live;
You can live as if nothing is a miracle,
Or you can live as if everything
Is a miracle."
----Albert Einstein

Miracles

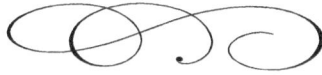

It's often been said that out of darkness grow miracles. It seems so when we witness so many people during their darkest times painfully praying for the faith to believe in them. Yet, I know miracles aren't only for people in pain.

What is a miracle? Throughout the ages there have been many different beliefs about them. For example, some believe miracles are a divine action that goes beyond what is normally perceived as a natural law and something man cannot produce, thereby, making a miracle a supernatural event. Is it possible that miracles are not conflicting to nature, but perhaps only what we do not understand about nature?

I remember visiting Disneyland as a child and hearing that someday we would be able to see people while we talked with them on the phone. My siblings and I laughed and skeptically stated, "Oh sure that's impossible!" But how many impossible things are we living with today? We landed a man on the moon, we have computers that can process infinite amounts of information, we have technology that can diagnose and treat conditions that were death sentences years ago. How many airplanes does one have to ride in until we no longer marvel how something so great and heavy can stay up in the air? Was Steve Jobs asking the impossible when he required his staff to create a reality out of his imagination?

If you read about miracles in the Bible, a miracle is an extraordinary event manifested by divine intervention and usually performed in front of multitudes so they could witness they were real. The Bible is full of stories about miracles that resisted explanation other than a supernatural event given to them through divine power. Many believe that miracles are no longer made known in today's world; they were meant only for those that lived while Jesus walked the earth. Yet, there are some people today who disagree, mainly because they have experienced them. Are they gigantic, like raising the dead, turning water into wine or perhaps walking on water? Skeptics, who don't believe now, probably wouldn't have believed back then either. Miracles are personal; they don't arrive in equal bundles and there are no requirements that they be earth shattering, quiet or subtle.

If God is logical and works within the realm of natural law, then is a miracle an unexpected and welcome event that man just hasn't found the scientific answer to yet, or is a miracle actually the work of divine intervention? I believe it's both because our existence alone is nothing short of a miracle. Every thought we think, every feeling we experience and every emotion we live are really comprehensibly impossible by our understanding, so how can we be anything less than a divine miracle? Yet, we tend to rationalize things. Prove something has scientific backing and then it becomes a simple truth, but show us something we don't understand and we will more than likely call it a miracle. How do we tell the difference?

How can we possibly know and understand everything there is to know about natural laws or science before we are thrown into a challenging life event we weren't expecting? Do we have all the knowledge and understanding to survive the kind of trials or tragedies that have the power to wipe us out? Many of us just haven't had the time or experience to become an Albert Einstein before we receive what we need to make it through difficult times. This is where the heavens step in to help us.

If we are blessed to experience and learn new things or witness events that help us grow in knowledge and understanding, then many things we used to consider mysterious or supernatural become a routine human experience. Whether we choose to label them as a mystery or a miracle is up to us. If we choose to open our eyes, and believe, we soon recognize that life is a continual series of miracles. Miracles surround us all the time. Maybe changing our perception of what a miracle is will enable us to actually see them.

I am beyond grateful when a miracle shows up, because many times they have the power to change my perception or help me get through something I believe I can't survive. Life is constantly changing and change can be painful or beautiful, but with the help of miracles we can learn our journey need not be traveled alone. Divine help is available to us simply because we are children of a loving God.

My definition of a miracle is an interaction between myself and Heaven. I think I would miss a lot if I had to understand the scientific reason why I experienced something. If one can receive, but need no proof, it would be easier to see that life is revealed to us one precious miracle at a time. To see, you must believe. Faith is required to believe, yet, as corny as this may sound good old common sense tries to convince us differently.

I have been blessed to believe and witness miracles, large and small, but I would like to share a story about one in particular that had a very comforting and profound effect on me.

My daughter Kris and her husband had bravely taken the steps to move over the mountains to a little unknown town in Eastern Oregon, where they bought a restaurant and embarked on becoming successful entrepreneurs. I witnessed the excitement as they took over and began to redo the interior, the menu and the character of the place. They were living a dream and I was happy for them.

The first year of ownership was approaching and Kris wanted to make their first Mother's Day a special one. We talked on the phone many times and she asked me to help her plan the menu for an elegant brunch, so we agreed to meet in Salem for breakfast to discuss our plans.

We went to a place we had visited often and my usual custom was to sit down next to her, but for some reason I chose to sit across from her. When I sat down, I noticed that her left eye was drooping and I expressed my concern that maybe she'd had a small stroke but didn't realize it. She assured me that it was only allergies and I shouldn't be concerned. Still I felt the urge to insist she get it checked out when she got home. She would try she said, even though she had a busy week ahead of her.

The week passed, I loaded my vehicle with all the things I told her I would gather together for the brunch, and headed over the mountains to her restaurant. When I arrived it was early Friday and we headed to town to do more shopping. We decided to go to lunch first and once again I sat across from her and noticed her eye had gotten worse. I asked if she had made an appointment to see a doctor, but she brushed it off calmly replying she just didn't have the time.

It was getting late when we unloaded the vehicles, and I informed her I needed to head out because I had reserved a cabin a few miles away for the night and because I wasn't familiar with the drive or the town I wanted to get there before dark. I arrived hungry and tired just as dusk was turning to night, and I soon realized that no stores, gas stations or restaurants were open. I found the cabin and was surprised it had electricity but nothing else. There was no television, no cell phone reception or Wi-Fi. I felt like a Pioneer; I couldn't even check my emails. I later learned that the cabins were designed for hunters who were perfectly satisfied having no modern conveniences. I reserved the cabin because it was the only lodging in the area and too tired to let it bother me, I just went to bed hoping for a good night's sleep. We had a lot to do the next day and I needed the rest. We were going to get the salads made, set up the buffet tables, and oversee the kitchen staff as they worked on the special menu. We were expecting a big crowd.

It was about 6 AM when I heard my cell phone ring. Surprised, I jumped out of bed and lunged to the desk where I had it plugged in. It was Kris, and she was struggling to speak. "Mom," she whimpered, "I think I fell and broke my ribs, I am in so much pain. Can you take me to the Emergency Room?"

"You fell?" I asked, wondering how in the heck she let that happen. "We're you drinking?"

"No," she cried, "I just walked out the door and for no reason I fell down and my side hit the rails on the steps. I don't understand what happened, can you please hurry because I'm about ready to pass out."

"I'm on my way," I told her, "Just stay put and try not to move too much." I said goodbye, ended the call and looked at the bars on my phone which still indicated I had no cell service.

On my drive to get her, the thought kept running through my mind that I needed to take advantage of the fact that she would actually be seeing a doctor, so I had to make sure I brought up the subject of her droopy eye. Her son helped her into the car and we headed to the ER.

It was busy, and no one seemed to think her case was urgent. I approached the counter a couple of times telling them that I thought she might have had a stroke. Still, we sat there for three hours before they finally called her in. The Doctor was frazzled, and apologized for the long wait. "These small hospitals are stingy with their doctors," she said, "I am the only one on duty and we are swamped."

Kris told her she fell, and thinks she broke some ribs. The doctor was in a hurry and just as quick as she walked in, she turned to leave. "I'll send someone in to take you to get an x-ray," she stated walking towards the door.

A powerful feeling grew stronger and stronger and I couldn't help but yell, "Wait!"

The doctor, somewhat startled by my outburst, turned and looked at me in surprise and snapped, "What?"

"I think she fell because something is going on in her brain." I pointed at Kris's eye, "Her eye has been drooping for quite a few days now, and I think she needs to get it checked out."

She turned to Kris, "Why do you think you fell?"

"I honestly don't know," replied Kris.

"Well it doesn't look concerning to me, a droopy eye doesn't necessarily mean there's something going on in the brain." She looked at me as if she wanted to tell me to back off and let her be the doctor.

This voice in my mind kept prompting me to push more, even though I knew the doctor was feeling rushed and frustrated. "I think you should do a CT scan just to be sure," I said. "Safe is always better than sorry."

The doctor's agitation moved up a couple notches. "We don't just do CT scans without a valid reason; insurance companies won't cover it if we do."

"If I have to," I responded with determination, "I'll pay for it." By then, I knew Kris had to have one. I didn't know why I knew, but I knew.

The doctor took a deep breath, anxious to be finished with the conversation. "Well fine" she said, "I guess I'll order a CT scan if you insist, but I don't think we need it." Then she left.

Kris looked at me, her eyes big as saucers. "Are you sure mom? Other than wishing someone would knock me out so I stop hurting, I think I will be fine."

"Hopefully you'll be fine and didn't break anything," I replied. "We'll just wait and hope it doesn't take another five hours before someone comes in to get you."

It wasn't long before someone arrived and took her away to x-ray and then in to get a CT scan. I was hoping it wouldn't be too long before results came back and hopefully we could be sent on our way. We had already been there too long and the day was getting away from us.

About thirty minutes passed before the doctor walked back through the door. Her demeanor had drastically changed and she didn't seem in a hurry. She pulled up a chair next to the Kris's bed and put her hand on her arm. She struggled to get the words out while I was beginning to feel anxiety rise. "Yes, you have broken a couple of ribs," she told her," however you have a much greater problem. The CT scan revealed that you have a tumor about the size of a lemon sitting is an extremely problematic spot in your brain. I have never seen the likes of anything resembling this one before. We are not a hospital capable of handling such things, and I do believe we need to find a hospital that can ASAP."

After the shock of hearing the news, I took a deep breath and asked, "You mean somewhere like OHSU, Oregon Health Science University?" OHSU was a research hospital which specialized in neurological issues and was about a hundred miles away.

"Yes," she replied compassionately as if she was feeling regretful for trying to brush us off so hurriedly before. "If you both agree, I will send for an ambulance to transfer her there."

Kris and I agreed and the doctor left. "I miss Lanette Mom, but I'm not ready to go be with her." She started to cry, "I don't want to die, my kids still need me."

I just kept holding her as the tears engulfed us. After insisting she get a CT scan, one would have thought that the news wouldn't have been such a shock, but it was and it felt like we were part of a bad dream that hopefully we would soon wake from.

I called her husband and two of her sons came with him to follow the ambulance to OHSU. It was late in the evening when I arrived back at their business where I let the help know what was going on. "Try as I may," I told them, "There is no way I'm physically or emotionally capable of pulling off the brunch on Sunday by myself, however I will figure something out that can make it special."

The next day, I prayed and waited to hear back about Kris. While I waited, I made a variety of small desserts that we could serve everyone who ordered dinner in honor of Mother's Day. Word had quickly traveled and the whole town was more concerned about Kris than whether or not there was going to be a special brunch, nothing but her health mattered.

I kept praying that the tumor not be malignant, and finally that afternoon her husband called and said that an MRI seemed to reveal that it wasn't malignant, however, it was very large and was beginning to wrap around her cardioid artery and they would have to operate before it completely shut off the blood supply to her brain.

The events of that week kept running through my mind until I realized that God had been speaking to me in a manner I could not ignore. I take no credit for insisting that she see a doctor, get a CT scan or anything else. I give all the credit to the miracle of God deciding that He would be heard.

Kris's surgery lasted over 18 hours. The doctors struggled because it was in a very difficult spot to reach and it was as they later explained a large rubbery mass that couldn't be completely removed but they got the part out that was life threatening. The good news was that it didn't appear to be malignant, however, they wouldn't know for sure until lab results were back. They assured us that had they not found it when they did, the possibility of her just dropping dead without warning was very real.

Kris struggled with overwhelming fear before going into surgery. She was afraid she wouldn't wake up and if she did, would her brain be so injured that she would end up disabled or mentally impaired?

A comforting sense of peace slowly engulfed me, and I had to share this with her. "Look at the events that have taken place," I said to her the night before her surgery, "Do you think God would have knocked you off your feet to get your attention if He didn't want you to live? How about me sitting across from you and noticing your eye or the fact that your call reached me where there was no cell service? What about that nagging feeling I had to insist on a CT scan? You are going to be ok that much I know! It has been witnessed to me and I have no doubt."

Kris has not gone without suffering painful side effects. The left side of her face is numb, making it hard to eat sometimes and her jaw is always in pain because many of the nerves attached to the tumor were disturbed, but hopefully time will heal those things. It's seems troublesome that she must keep a close eye on the tumor to make sure it isn't growing, but miraculously she is alive and she is still the Kris we love and cherish. She is also just as beautiful a person as she always was. All these events, she admits, has helped her grow spiritually. She remarks often how she sees things through a new set of eyes. "It's amazing she says, "I see God's hand in more things these days. She's not alone because many others have come to know the reality of miracles through their trials.

Was my experience a miracle? My perception tells me it was absolutely a miracle. It may have been a miracle only my soul could see until I was ready to share it, but that is how miracles are sometimes, quiet, subtle, yet sure.

Until one is ready to open their eyes to the possibility of miracles, it is more than likely that they will miss them one by one as they parade by in plain view. Disbelief can drift into our thoughts causing us to always question the possibility of anything we don't have a logical answer for. We can say we were cured because of the skilled hands of a surgeon, not God. However, if you asked that surgeon why he chose to be a doctor, he might say an experience in his life inspired him to become one. Where does inspiration come from?

People aren't as shy these days about talking about miracles. It's easy to claim a miracle has happened when the results are good...like health restored, an accident prevented or finding a long lost loved one, so surely God must have intervened. Sometimes we tend to over generalize the topic as if everything good happens because of a miracle and everything bad happens because of evil. I would caution against such illogical thinking because it takes away from the divine reasons for real ones. Sometimes a trial happens and it ends up being the catalyst that leads us to God.

It's good to be delivered from danger in a supernatural way, or be healed when it seemed impossible, and yes, to some it probably was a miracle, but how can we tell the difference?

Discerning between a miracle and wishful thinking requires a little conscious work. Having a mind that's clear and spiritually fine-tuned can help us know the difference, because many times miracles come in the form of inspiration, gentle whispers and sacred understanding? We also need spiritual vision? A mind that is spiritually tuned in and eyes that can see are both essential to bring us a truly touching experience. Working on our awareness helps the deepest part of our thoughts understand things that might otherwise be unfamiliar or strange to us. A true desire for truth will help us discern the difference. Prayer and desire are wonderful first steps to take.

I find miracles to be the runway lights that help us see while we travel difficult roads. When we travel through adversity, we usually have our eyes focused on the problem rather than the God who is always in control. Without knowing all the answers, miracles help us know that He has a purpose and plan which is sometimes beyond our understanding.

It's ok to believe in miracles even if you never have. I hope that you can condition your spiritual eyes to see the wonders and blessings that surround you. I hope you can condition your spirituality so you may feel the peace and hope of every message you receive from Heaven. Think of the word, supernatural. What does it really mean? Super…meaning wonderful, natural…meaning normal, Supernatural: Wonderfully Normal.

When a miracle appears, it breaks through the darkness as a ray of light, let it teach you and bring you peace

Find the guide
For building and repair
So you may accept your mission here.
Find the tools strong enough
To hold the mold,
But made of power
And spiritual gold.

Tools

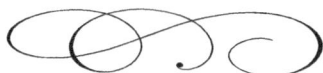

You have a job to do and you may ask yourself, "Where do I begin?" It's a job because like many other worthwhile projects, there will be a payoff, a reward, or a currency that will be in direct proportion to the amount of effort and skill invested in it. Many professions usually require an education and tools that are specifically designed to complete the work. Getting through grief, no matter what the reason, will probably be one of the most challenging tasks you will ever take on because there's a chance you didn't go to college to learn how to prepare for it, and it's likely you have to hustle to find the knowledge, resources, and tools to get on with the task before it disables your ability to function.

Think of all the definitions we can attach to the word tools. There are several different types such as: technical ones to help us understand all the new technology that bombards us on a daily basis, physical ones that help us craft and create physical objects such as hammers, screwdrivers, or machinery. There are business tools to help us facilitate the carrying out of a particular type of business, such as marketing tools, management tools, intellectual tools—this list could go on forever, but we know that tools are things to help us carry out a number of projects or vocations.

Visualize that you are entering a shop, a garage, or a specific location where you are going to locate the necessary tools to start on a project. You're not quite sure what you will need, but you believe you have a fair idea, so you begin your search. You've determined the task, located the shop, now you are entering it, and you have the intention of putting together a fairly functional box of tools. Before you can go too far, however, you need a decent overhead light to take inventory of what is available to you. Because your project is so personal, you will need to carefully evaluate what is under the light because you know that your success depends on the tools you choose. However, if you are new to the work and not quite sure of what you need to complete the task, you will need to understand the purpose of each tool.

You are probably standing at that workbench in a state of numbness, pain, or confusion, and now, you need tools—but which ones do you choose? The fact is most of us don't know where to begin that's why we need some type of light shed on the process, either by others who have been there or by some type of spiritual understanding.

A grief first aid kit will help you know where to begin. What's the difference between a toolbox and a first aid kit? Think about what you do when you or someone around you has incurred an injury that could be life threatening. You don't usually have the luxury of grabbing a book or enrolling in an online or college course to know the most educated way to give immediate attention to the injury. A first aid kit is to bridge the gap between hanging on until help arrives or healing begins.

So let's build a first aid kit! The first thing in our kit is to ask for light and inspiration so you will recognize the tools that will help you heal. Even though your eyes may be full of tears, it may be something as simple as looking up to the heavens and asking for help, then take whatever faith or desire you have, a lot or very little, and add it to the kit. Don't worry; a seed of faith will grow. You'll be surprised how illuminated the process of moving forward will be with your choice.

When you have realized a desire to heal, to stop hurting, and to feel joy again in spite of what may seem an impossible hurdle to get over, allow yourself the right to hurt, to stumble, and sometimes to fall backward. Add patience to the kit. No matter what, you deserve patience, in fact; add a little more than you think you need and refuse to let anyone take an ounce away from you. It's very easy for those standing on the sidelines that have not walked in your shoes to decide it is time for you to let go. The next thing to add to the kit is a promise that you will be kind to yourself while trying to locate and implement the tools to regain your emotional balance. An understanding of this will have a profound effect on both your physical and emotional health, not only in the present, but in the future as well.

Be cautious not to deceive yourself into believing that because your pain is so intense you have the right to stay stuck in it forever—desire to get unstuck! I also want to caution you to be on guard about the allure of using substances like drugs and alcohol to medicate the pain, even momentarily, because both clothe themselves in deceptive illusions and you could easily become convinced that they are an easier fix to keep you from dealing with your pain or feelings. They not only separate you from reality, but lead to addictions and fear, plus they keep you from acknowledging that your goal is to heal and experience a life of wellness. Medicating yourself with substances convinces you of the big lie that the journey to healing is impossible, and it is not. Your goal should be to achieve understanding on how to balance you mind, body, and spirit so you may have a healthy state of wellness. Wellness is a powerful word and probably the least understood. It is the goal of any type of emotional or grief work. Wellness is the optimal health and goal for living a higher quality of life. What you say to yourself and what you think is at the core of emotional health.

The next thing to add to your kit is balance. Of all the times in your life where you will need to tip the scales in your favor between work, family, and self will be in the life-altering moments when you are trying to take care of this first aid moment to save your life—until healing begins, shift the weight to your side. You deserve it and you are worth it!

When you have your first aid kit in place, you will recognize and rejoice in the tools presented in this book to help you not only heal your wound, but also in presenting hands on ways to balance all aspects of your life as well as regaining well-being and purpose.

Of all the things that I could wish for you and anyone else who must suffer a great loss or trauma in their lives is to know where to peacefully place the event in your heart where at times you can tap into and respect it as something that helped bring you into greater understanding of life, compassion, empathy, and your own value.

The following chapters I refer to as tools encompass both hands-on doing and emotional and spiritual understanding. Knowing something in your heart can be just as powerful as physically doing something because this creates the awareness inside that is capable of physically changing the amount of energy you generate toward your healing.

Journal:

It's been a year and about three months since Lanette died. It seems like yesterday. I have been through two Christmases and at least one of every holiday. I can't believe I survived any of them! Christmas was five days ago, and our trip to Las Vegas to spend Christmas with my in-laws was like an episode of The Twilight Zone. My family flew there the day before Christmas, so afterward, my Mother and Father in-law could drive us home and spend a couple of days with us in Arizona. The holiday was difficult to get through because the void created by Lanette's absence not only brought on memories that made my heart ache, but it was as obvious as that familiar elephant sitting on my chest. We headed home in the late afternoon the day after Christmas and the long desolate stretch of the highway between Las Vegas and our home seemed like my life. How was I going to finish raising my children when I felt so lost in the desert?

My Father-in-law was driving and I was sitting in the backseat with my Husband and Daughter, Kristy. We sat in sad stillness as darkness began to consume everything except for the light of a Burger King off in the distance. I stared at the sign as we approached it and began the very familiar habit of recalling memories. We had stopped at that Burger King on a trip to Vegas the summer before Lanette's death, and in the excitement of being able to get out of the car and stretch her legs, Lanette started to run and instantly took a nosedive into the gravelly blacktop of the parking lot. She skinned both knees and managed to get a couple of pebbles lodged in the palm of her hand. She wanted to be so grown and independent, yet she turned and lunged toward me in a barrage of tears for the comfort that only a mother could give a child who wanted the pebbles removed and a shoulder to cry on..

The memory returned me to the day she died and the realization that her last day on earth was not a day I could kiss the pain away or remove a couple of pebbles from her hand. It launched me into an onslaught of *tears that caught the attention of my Father-in-law. He jerked his head around to look at me in a tense response to my tears, and exhaling a deep breath, he irritably stated it had been more than a year and it was time for me to just let it go.*

Perhaps one of my greatest lessons about grief and one of the things that should be added to the first aid kit is the understanding that grief is not something you decide one day to just let go of. It is also not something that you just get over, but something that you have to work right through the heart of. Grieving is such a personal experience, and a time stamp has not been put on it nor a set of rules that apply to all. Depending on you and your situation or the nature of your loss, your journey through the storm will be different from another person's, and this is why I say do not let someone push you into their expected time frame, because there is no normal and there is no set of rules. Just try to understand that while people may think they are helping, they are not walking in your shoes and their heart is not beating in your chest. Sometimes, they just do not know better.

I have put the tools in your tool box, and I pray that they will help you build and repair your life.

If you have a song, sing it.
If you have a deed, do it.
If the road appears, travel it.
If you find your purpose, live it.
If you feel love, share it.
If you feel pain, learn from it.

Life
A Tool of Understanding

L ife is real. It is not a theory, a personal philosophy, or a debate whether it exists. You are here and so am I—alive and living on this earth. It is not a man-made theory or a hypothetical idea that came about from either a believer of one thing or a nonbeliever of another—life literally exists and that is a fact. However, there is much conjecture and many different opinions and theories as to the whys and how's of it all, but not about the evidence of it.

Since we know we are alive, wouldn't it make sense to believe it is for a reason? Yet why can it be so difficult? The truth about life is that it is difficult, but it is also good. Have you ever listened to someone who just couldn't believe that something so tragic, sad, or disappointing could be happening to them? I have sat in support groups and observed shocked people who couldn't believe they had suddenly become part of the "it only happens to others" gathering. It's a normal reaction because before tragedy strikes, most people have this inner confidence that they will be the elect few who are chosen to escape such things. It is just human nature. Until the need arrives for us to reach deep down inside and muster the strength to survive, we may continually wish we were in a dream we could wake from. It may take reality a while to hit us, but until it does, we usually cry and beg to know "why me" as if our afflictions are hurled upon us by a cruel unnatural act from the forces that control the world.

If man is meant to have joy, why is there suffering in the world? Problems, depending upon their nature, can invite a myriad of emotions and grief, such as sadness, guilt, anger, despair, and many others, causing us great discomfort and physical pain. It is because of these events, which at some point in each life, no one escapes completely, we might have to admit, "Life is difficult." So then why not ask: "What's the point?" or "What's so great about life anyway?"

The wisdom of life lies in understanding, combined with action. It is really the process of learning from our problems that can give our life meaning. Problems do not go away nor can they be ignored for long. If we try to avoid them, no matter how, we create barriers to our growth and development, even to the point where our spirits shrivel. It takes discipline to solve problems, yet it is with complete resolve and dedicated discipline that, ultimately, we can solve all problems, whether on a personal level or on a humanity level. Yet it is from climbing those mountains and reaching the top that we also grow in courage and wisdom. Without experiencing life, we cannot grow. Sooner or later, if we can accept that our life is a series of personal choices and decisions, we gain the wisdom to know that from our choices and the lessons we gain we can actually discover true joy. At some time in each life, people will find themselves lost in some kind of wilderness where the light of God can appear like rain on a parched desert or air to someone gasping for oxygen or manna from heaven. As it was in the Bible days, the history of life is as much yours as mine. We may all experience some type of wilderness so we can learn that if we look up, help is there.

We were designed and created magnificently like a unique work of art with nothing less than having great value. Our Creator knows that our lives are works in progress for the express purpose of achieving our full potential. So what does value mean? Value means having great worth. The opposite of worth is useless, fruitless, unimportant, disrespected. There is nothing created that is worthless. It is actually our moral responsibility to not be deceived by appearances, not even good ones, beautiful ones, or weak ones. We must look beyond what the world or deviant minds want us to believe beauty is or what value is because such things can be deceiving. Getting caught up in deception can make things even more difficult. There is truth in knowing that every life possesses value, beauty, and the essence of light.

So what about all those who appear to have no direction, no morals, or who make bad choices that end up hurting others? It's hard to wrap your mind around that question, but still, God has not created one life that is of no value. It's hard to believe when we have been a victim of someone's bad choices or witnessed pain and suffering brought on by the evil intentions of others, but without complete understanding of each and every person's life and trials, we've been admonished not to judge for we do not know the circumstances of the world in which they were raised, their family background, or their individual challenges. We send people to prison to keep them from hurting others, and sometimes, we put them to death because they have offended beyond the ability of what society can handle, yet it is still their Creator who knows all from the beginning to the end. Free agency has given men the choice to make good or bad choices, and yet, to be on this earth and to live on this earth, we have to live with the whole creation, not just the nice parts, and there is no doubt that evil does live among us, which is one of the reasons that laws exist. Laws help us live as safely as we can in spite of everything.

The material world hides behind masks that we don't always understand, and in our search for peace, some of us tend to feel cursed with all the confusing thoughts that riddle our mind. It is easy to feel as if God has forsaken us when we question why he doesn't remove anguish, grief, depression, or war and crime from our lives. Even with all these questions, a fact remains: all of God's children were created with value and purpose.

It would be wonderful if we could teach our children self- esteem so they know that they are valued simply because they exist. Feelings of inadequacy, lack of self-respect and self-love are sadly apparent in sweeping percentages in our world. Our mental illness industry is saturated with people who feel they are undeserving of love and happiness. So imagine when they suffer a loss in their life or experience an event that can cripple them either emotionally or physically, some actually feel it was either their fault or they were singled out because of their lack of value or their worthiness to heal.

Every person comes to earth with a mission to fulfill. Do we fail sometimes? Yes, some do, and sadly, many lives are taken before their appointed time has been fulfilled. Life is a reality that comes with man's free agency to choose his behavior. Does it end all life? No, it can't and it's a good thing to understand that because only our Creator knows when a life has left us because it was their appointed time or because free agency cut it short. It takes a lot of courage to change your belief system if you believe that you are not valuable and worthy of a life of peace.

Your belief paradigm will guide you through your life's journey. It is your responsibility to make a shift if you want the outcome to be conducive to healing. Try to make the shift to understand that you are a wonderful creation of a compassionate, loving Creator, and you have a purpose and a reason to be here. One's quality of life is the sum total of every choice and every decision they make. Theodore Roosevelt, the twenty-sixth president of the United States and a Nobel Peace Prize winner, spoke often about the challenges of life and learning how to have the courage to do something instead of nothing even if you don't have the strength. In order to succeed, realizing we are living in an arena called life is where we can begin to understand the importance of it.

"In the battle of life it is not the critic who counts; not the man who points out how the strong stumbled, or where the doer of a deed could have done better. The credit belongs to the man who is actually in the arena; whose face is marred by dust and sweat and blood; who strives valiantly, who errs and comes short again and again because there is no effort without error and shortcoming; who does actually strive to do the deeds; who knows the great enthusiasm, the great devotions, spends himself in a worthy cause; who at the best knows in the end the triumph of high achievement; and who at the worst if he fails, at least fails while daring greatly, so that his place shall never be with those cold timid souls who knew neither victory nor defeat. " 3
—Theodore Roosevelt

There are many who, because of fear or laziness, want to be shown every inch of the way that their life and every step they take will be a safe one— even one worth their precious time. How can this be done? The journey of growth is not one that comes with guarantees or even the ability to see around those narrow winding roads. No one else can travel your journey. No teacher, church, or specific group can carry you. There are no preset formulas. Teachers can be inspiring and rituals can be learning aides, but only traveling the paths, choosing the course, and trying to live toward understanding your own unique circumstances while moving forward into the light will get you to your destination.

Why is the value of your life crucial to understanding in the process of grief? Does it make you hurt any less or miss your loved one any less? Grief hurts, and the void in your life when someone has been there and is suddenly gone is not easy to deal with, even if that someone had moved across the world and you were unable to see them on a daily basis, you would still miss them. The importance of knowing how valuable you are is so you will realize that your loved one's life is also valuable and because they have made a transition from this earth to the next realm of God's plan gives us the comfort of knowing that God doesn't create value just to end it with death. If there is any one thing that gives me hope it is this: we go on after death. Man's spirit is endless.

Even though death may seem unfair and those left behind have wounds to deal with, it really is as much a part of life as breathing. What we do today will largely depend on what we do tomorrow, and what we have done in the past year marks our path as to what we will do the next. Day by day, hour by hour, we travel our road, we build our lives, and we learn valuable lessons that hopefully will build us into better people and give us a sense of our greater purpose as we mark off one by one the passing years? What is one of our greatest purposes? To cherish life, to understand our soul, and to be a light that will endure and brighten other's paths we cross while on this earth and throughout eternity. Our journey is here and now. Life is before us, not only this earthly life, but an eternal one. Both of them are tied together by a golden thread that runs like perfect artwork through the tapestry of who we are.

Before your life took physical form, you existed. I offer this as a window that you can look through long enough to ask for the light to come through and touch that part of you that will recognize its truth. We are multi-sensory human beings, and unless we seek out the ability to tap into all our senses, many of us stumble through life, trying to survive with only the five senses of sight, smell, taste, touch, and hearing.

We are both students and teachers in this life; our knowledge of the world around us depends a great deal on our willingness to learn and our mode of perception. If you thought for a moment you were not tapping into all the sensory gifts you were created with, wouldn't you want to find out how you could get them to kick in and function? Most people function at a primitive level and don't give much thought of appreciation about one of their five senses until one is taken away. Why is this important to bring to light? It is important because sometimes, it is a good idea to stop for a moment and look at things differently.

Imagine you were born blind and someone was trying to describe to you a sunset. Do you think if you were suddenly given sight and were able to see a sunset that you would recognize it the way your mind painted the picture? It has been shown that when a blind person became sighted, they were not able to recognize what their mental pictures had created because they had no point of reference or anything to compare it with.

Imagine someone was born without a sense of smell, do you think that you would be able to imagine the scent of a rose just by touching it? A person born without one sense has no conception what they are missing by replacing it with another sense. Touch cannot make you smell or even recreate what smell is. Perhaps if you experienced smell once before and lost it, your memory could produce a good feeling of what it was once like.

We are entering into a new age of understanding in many ways because people are stopping to pay attention to those things that go beyond their five senses. Unless you personally experience it, you can't completely describe it to someone. A multi-sensory person's experiences and understandings of physical, spiritual and scientific experiences are so much more illuminated. A multi-sensory person's consciousness pertaining to the physical world and the spiritual world is not limited to only what their physical eyes can see. So how can I tell you how a rose smells if you have never had the sense of smell?

If you want to understand your spirit and the fact that it exists, would you consider tapping into a new sense, one you weren't aware was there? If you were armed with a new sense, a window of light, what do you suppose you would see that you didn't see before? What will you miss if you refuse to let the light in? If you tapped into all of your senses, what secrets do you suppose you could uncover? What view of the universe would you see? When you get it, you will feel like the blind man who was just given sight and a whole new view of the universe, your purpose and your Creator will be in full view before you.

So I repeat, why are we here and what is our purpose for living, and why do some have to leave and some have to stay behind? The purpose of every person who comes to earth is to experience life in the physical form and to learn whatever lessons are individual to each soul. We all have our own personalities, and if we can learn how to connect with our soul, we will begin to achieve balance, the kind that can help make our time here more productive and more joyful.

We come to the earth as children, and as we grow, we learn life lessons that only experiencing it can teach us and such is our life as a whole; hopefully, we will learn lessons of the spirit such as love, compassion, service, and through all of our experiences, including sorrow, how to connect back to our true authentic God-made self.

Try looking at your life as a beautifully and intelligently created force, therefore, trusting that your experiences and circumstances are working toward your best and most appropriate never- ending life. Let the light in and ask for guidance to let you know where you need to be and then trust in God and the universe to provide for you. Seek to let go of all that stands in your way so that your higher multi-sensory self can complete its task and give your life more meaning. Be a lighthouse unto yourself and to the world, and never lose or underestimate your importance. Sometimes, our vision can become hazy and unclear, but you are made by God, and his essence manifests itself in you. This is a truth, embrace it.

A Love driven life
Is not blinded by a need
To compare and keep score.
It can transform and teach,
Inspiring one to become or move to explore.
However joyful or powerfully sweet,
Love without service and compassion,
Remains elusive and incomplete.

Love
A Tool of Understanding and Doing

One warm September evening in 2001, three police officers stopped beside the freeway to help a Washington family heading home from the Oregon coast when their van broke down on Interstate 5, just north of Albany. One officer was a thirty-nine-year-old female Oregon State Police Senior Trooper, another was a forty-one-year-old Oregon State Patrol Sergeant, and the other was a twenty-nine-year-old off-duty Albany Police Officer who welcomed the chance to ride along that day with the Sergeant he considered his mentor. They all stood on the grass next to the highway with their patrol cars parked to provide a barrier between them and the traffic, discussing where to take the family for the night. Abruptly, out of the blue, a small pickup truck veered off the road and slammed into them. The driver of the truck was an exhausted nineteen-year-old college student who had fallen asleep at the wheel after spending most of the day driving home from a church camp in California. His truck clipped one of the patrol cars, and slammed into the officers. The female officer and the young off-duty officer were killed instantly, and the Sergeant suffered a devastating brain injury. A week later, the national tragedy of 9/11 would overshadow the terrible accident, but the effects of it were felt by Oregonians for years to come.

My partner and I had received the call requesting our services to show up on the scene to transport the two deceased officers to the state medical examiner's facility. By the time we arrived, it was late and the news vans, investigators, and several state troopers were beginning to leave, and the ones remaining were ready to help us clear the scene. The atmosphere was heartrending; it had been an extremely taxing night and everyone was exhausted as they worked in reverent silence. The well-loved and respected female officer had been thrown and entangled in a chain link fence that paralleled with the freeway. When we were given the okay clear the scene, we assessed the task at hand and discussed how we were going to free her from the twisted fence. We silently placed the cot next to her and began the tedious task of compassionately untangling her. We had just begun when four of her fellow officers asked if they could please have the honor of freeing her from the fence and placing her on the cot. They also requested that they be able to carry her to the vehicle. They wept as they gently and tenderly freed her from the tangled fence. There was no doubt they all shared a special kind of love and respect for her. After they lovingly moved her and put her in the vehicle, they turned their attention to the young Albany Officer and humbly did the same thing for him. Love was present, and it was evident that hearts were broken that night.

A few days later, they had a service for the female officer in the Salem Armory with a procession to the cemetery planned afterward. We were asked to be in the procession and, in her honor, to turn on our flashing emergency lights while we drove. This was a new experience for me and I had no idea what to expect. The armory was packed and hundreds stood outside of the building to pay their respects. It took quite a while for the procession to the cemetery to start because of the number of honoring vehicles that had to line up. There were officers from every county, every city, and many other states. Every fire department was represented and every city sent a car. It was overwhelming, but not as profound as the people that lined the streets. They stood with their hands over their hearts or in a salute stance as her casket passed by. Because so many showed up, the procession lasted for miles.

Even though my partner was always telling me it wasn't professional to show emotion, I couldn't hold back the tears, I had to cry. I was witnessing such a large outpouring of love, and I gratefully had to acknowledge that we have so much more love in the world than we realize. Businesses shut down, people stayed home from work, and families gathered together to honor and thank this young lady for her dedicated service and her ultimate sacrifice. She was the only Oregon female State Trooper killed in the line of duty. You could reach out and literally touch the love in the air that day. The young nineteen-year-old Oregon State University student pleaded guilty to negligent homicide and apologized to the families, but when he heard they had forgiven him, he wept. The judge gave him community service hours, which was served doing public speaking on the dangers of tired or negligent driving. The families, heroes in their own right, agreed that to ask the judge to throw the book at him could potentially ruin his life and they didn't want to do that. They agreed that to understand and implement love ,regardless of the circumstances, they had to forgive him even though they knew he absolutely should not have driven to the point of exhaustion, however, they had to admit that in the end it was just a terrible accident. They chose to honor those they lost with a memory of love.

So what about love? What wouldn't we do for someone we love! We run into burning buildings to rescue them, we travel great miles to see them, and we give of our time and talents to help them. We write songs for them; we sing for them, inherently, we move mountains for them. We cry for them, we laugh with them, and we grieve as if our hearts are not strong enough to live without them.

It's true—people give and risk their lives every day for someone they love, but what is love? Really, what is love? What is that little four-letter word that we give so many accolades to? It can seem like an enigma if we try hard to analyze it. Some will tell you it's a feeling; some will say it's the glue that makes relationships work, the attraction of romance or the virtue of selflessness or simply life-giving essence. There is truth if you want to attach sensations that love gives us, yet that isn't all there is to it, and for such a small word, it packs in all the meaning of life.

If you want to navigate through your grief and you desire to travel the journey of your life without fear, you will need to understand love, and when you understand just enough to seek to understand, it will only be a matter of time until you begin living in the light. Even the smallest, most infinitesimal step forward at the beginning will have profound results in your life. God knows that reuniting with love is the supreme goal on earth. He makes it available, but it doesn't always come easy.

A Legitimate Journey

For many, suffering the death or loss of a loved one, they are instantly hurled into a state of fear. Fear is great at spawning countless scary thoughts such as: how will I ever be able to live without them, happiness and joy will now forever be a thing of the past, I will never be able to laugh again, life will never hold any meaning for me, or I will never be able to trust or to believe again. The long list of emotions generated by fear can be disabling. Depression is a very common ailment associated with the fear that grief produces and everyone knows how debilitating depression can be. It doesn't seem fair, does it?

Love has a deep spiritual meaning, the kind capable of bringing balance and healing into your life. If you understand it, you will have within your grasp one of the most powerful tools available to help you through your grief.

Most of us have been taught that the opposite of love is hate— it is not. The absence of love is fear. Most negative emotions, which we all know we experience more than ever in grief, originate out of fear. I used to worry that if I were ever to laugh again, it would be a betrayal of the love I had for my child. I feared that if she were watching from heaven, it would make her think I didn't love her as much as I said I did. Fear has energy, love has energy, and behind your actions or your thoughts, one or the other is at work. Fear is the energy that fuels negative emotions and love is the energy that fuels positive emotions.

Most think of love as the tender affection we have for someone in our life or the admiration for family and friends or the respect we give to others who do good or make us feel good, but it goes beyond that. Love is the language that communicates with your spirit stronger than anything else. It is the reason that the world was created. It is packed into every gift that has been given to man on earth. It is the light in the room, it is in the hand we reach out to a hungry stranger, it is a beautiful sunset, a fragile rose, and it is in the tears we cry to wash our soul. It is literally the essence of life.

Love is not a feeling, because a feeling is an emotion, and emotions can come and go with the wind. Emotions can be exciting, passionate, warm, even hateful, sorrowful, fearful, and prideful. If you look up love in the dictionary, you will find a long list of what the author has determined the meaning of love to be. Most of the definitions have to do with an emotion. In Webster's Ninth Collegiate Dictionary, the list starts with: strong affection for another arising out of kinship or personal ties or attraction based on sexual desire, affection and tenderness felt by lovers, affection based on admiration, benevolence, common interests, warm attachment, enthusiasm, devotion and about half way down the list is: unselfish loyal and benevolent concern for the good of another. This last one is closer to the definition than those that preceded it. Genuine love is an action, a conscious choice, a determination, and decision for the purpose of nurturing one's own spiritual growth and that of other's as well. It is in our DNA to be hungry if we do not have love. The person who loves does so because of a decision to. Love is a choice and finding it is in the blueprint of our creation; it is the divine force within us that teaches us to extend ourselves for the sake of growth, it is the force that enlightens us, and it is the force that nudges us to move and act against the inertia of laziness to serve, to work, and to exercise courage. Love does not exist without work or courage. If you want to understand happiness, understand that to love completely and generously, you are making yourself a gift to others. If love is an action, then these should be the characteristics that define it: Free choice, a gift of self, eternal, and life-giving. Every miraculous moment of your life you are either choosing love or fear.

Love is that light within you that will manifest the truth. As children of God, we are created by love and for love. We are the only creatures called to the pursuit of it. This sets us apart from the animals and plant kingdom. Some people grow without being taught to understand and safeguard their ability to love, and therein, I believe lies much of our mental illness. From birth to death, love is the life force of the mind, our spirit, and our physical body, and to deny or not understand it leads us into unhappy unhealthy relationships and lack of self-worth, yet it is there still to be found and to be understood, it can still make us better and can take us out of laziness into action.

We were not created to live without love. We need love in our life. It's been said that unloved people die. People need touch, caring, and someone to listen to them. Love gives people a purpose in life and it gives them support.

It is challenging to understand and to become loving human beings in spite of the dark and confusing things we are subjected to. We came from a place of light where we knew and understood, yet it was our choice to be subjected to this testing existence for a higher purpose of understanding and evolution. Spiritual growth is the evolution of the individual.

I've watched as people have had to hand their infant back over to God and, like myself, had to say good-bye to a child that I loved beyond myself and wondered if joy was ever going to be a possibility. I've watched families grieve over seemingly senseless losses and wondered if they could survive the pain. When you see people consumed with grief, it's easy to believe love's essence has been lost, never to return, but it is an invisible life-giving force and I can tell you it doesn't get lost, it sometimes just doesn't get used.

To understand spiritual love is to be love. To understand it is to live your life unrestricted without the boundaries of human weaknesses. The difference between human love and spiritual love is that as humans, we still have the frailties that can challenge our effectiveness, but this is where I repeat that love takes work and courage and the more we exercise it, the better we get. However, whether it is human or spiritual, it all comes from the one source, God, and all that comes from God is eternal.

So what happens when we fall in and out of love, or we realize our love has turned into a negative experience. It could be family disagreements, cruelty or someone simply getting tired of dealing with the challenges some relationships present and therefore enabling love to become dormant. Difficult people can be hard to love, and most of us will know someone like that at least once during our life. Retraining our hearts to understand that we love because it is our nature to love and it is how we desire to be in the world— not because others deserve it or don't deserve it. However, the question remains about how to deal with difficult relationships or people that try to bring us down, criticize, and continually sabotage us with their negative energy. We can't always control, inspire, or will better behavior from others. There are times it is out of our hands and we simply need to distance ourselves from them, because not doing so could be unhealthy. We do not need to be unkind, mean, or angry, but we also owe ourselves the self-respect that our value deserves.

I recall the time I ended up in the intensive care unit of the hospital with heart issues brought about by stress. I was beside myself with worry over my teenage daughter and her emotional and defiant behavior, but the continual berating and emotional bullying I was receiving from a close family member was affecting my physical health more than I realized. I knew I needed to figure out how to let go of some things, but it was easier said than done. As I lay in bed, I remember fretting over how on earth one lets go of negative people who are connected by family ties. Did I have that right? The stress of that dilemma was part of what landed me in the hospital. If I removed that person from my life, it would affect my children, my mate, and even me because I cared about her. I knew I didn't have the power to change her behavior because for years, I believed if I just ignored the insults and tried to be nice, it would get better, but it only escalated year after year until I knew I deserved better.

In thoughtful reverie about my problem, hooked to a hundred wires and the continual beep of the monitors, I decided to turn the television on. That's when a miracle happened. Wayne Dyer was being interviewed, promoting his new book, *You'll See It When You Believe It*, and the host asked him how to handle difficult people in life. I remember his response as if it were yesterday. He said that if the people you associate with regularly are not a member of your fan club, wish them love, and move on without them.

What was it Dr. Dyer once said? "When the student is ready, the teacher will appear." I was a willing and ready student that day, and making a healthy decision wasn't as difficult as I thought it would be. I only expected myself to let go, no one else, because it was my health, my life, and therefore, my choice. I chose not to be a part of family visits, and when she came around, I would politely take leave. I refused to subject myself to the abuse. I had the choice—I always had the choice. Amazingly, I was set free without the guilt that would have typically eaten me alive before. We can love, but doing so does not require us to be abused. It is easy to love the lovable, and it is easy to love those that love you, but even stepping back from those who are hurtful does not justify mean-spiritedness or anger. It is learning to love all in the world that our greater power arises within us. It is important to remember that we can love without compromising our safety or self-respect. We can learn to love from a distance. It's important to remember that even those people who are difficult to deal with are important teachers in our life. If nothing else, they can teach us how we do not want to be. There are people in the world that may appear to lack redeeming qualities, yet they play a role in teaching us that they are also weaved from the fiber of God. When these kinds of people arise in your life, it is best to let them go and graciously move on. Try not to dwell on the pain they caused because dwelling on it too long will only make you feel like they are still standing next to you and jabbing you in the ribs, which, by the way, is where your heart is. It is crucial to separate yourself from their behavior. We all deserve to be treated with kindness.

When I was released from the hospital, the doctor said to me, "I don't know what is going on in your life, but you better go home and figure out how to change it because if you don't, you will not live long!"

Then one of them, which was a lawyer, asked him a question, tempting him and saying, Master, which is the great commandment in the law? Jesus said unto him, Thou shalt love the Lord they God with all thy heart, and with all thy soul, and with all they mind. This is the first and great commandment. And the second is like unto it, Thou shalt love they neighbor as thyself.
Matthew 22:35 (kjv)

Understanding this scripture can be applied to human problems. All laws lean upon the law of love. If love then is the greatest commandment and the basis for a successful life, wouldn't it be reasonable to say that its absence would cause unhappiness in a person's life? Would it be sound to assume that love's presence would lead someone to a sense of well-being and good mental health?

What does it really mean to love one's fellowman? The words are meaningless until it is demonstrated in distinct ways. There are two parts to love and both are crucial. To a loving spirit, the feeling and the doing are inseparably attached. When an unloving person goes through the motions without feeling love in his heart, the deed may be appreciated, but the other person will not feel the love. The true experience of love is that it blesses the one who gives and the one who receives. You can love, but if it isn't returned, you can't control it. There will be no doubt, however, if it is returned.

Love warms the soul and expands the heart. It gives us the courage to make our lives better and hope for a sense of peace. When a loving helpful person reaches out to someone in need, healing begins. Without love, men fear, they quarrel, and usually put a price tag on everything they do. Love should not carry a price tag.

Choosing to love can be insulation from some of life's worst blows. Its presence is a powerful tool to have available in so many of life's battles. The absence of love is painful and can be destructive. Love is doing, and when you do it, you can expect it to grow stronger day by day. When you reach out to those around you or become engaged in worthy causes even amidst your own pain, you will begin to see the healing balm of love at work on a deep spiritual level.

George G. Ritchie, MD, who wrote the book about his afterlife experience in *A Return from Tomorrow,* worked for many years as a psychiatrist afterward trying to help people navigate through trials in their lives and he came to a profound conclusion throughout the course of his work and his own near-death experience and ended his book by saying that he believes God is busy building men who know how to love. The fate of the world and man depends largely on the progress we make. Our time is very short in connection with how much there is to do and how much need remains. He believes that what we will find on the other side will depend on how well we get on with the business of loving here and now.

When we reunite with our maker, he will not ask us to account for all the wealth, fame, or material things that we were able to accrue, nor will he ask us how many times we had to slow down for those annoying speed bumps in our life. I am also convinced he will not ask for a detailed record of how many times someone hurt us, made us cry, or provoked us into anger. He won't need an explanation about how going through a tragedy or loss made our life go downhill from that point. It is my belief that God will simply ask, "How much did you love with the precious time I gave you?" You see, he will know that those who learned to love and love well would have had what they needed to weather the storms, amass their fortunes, and experience their life joyfully and harmoniously. He has given us everything we need to learn, to understand, and to handle what life dishes out. Could we not ask for more?

When we are in a state of grief for whatever the reason, the pressures of the world can seem impossible to deal with. If we are not careful, we can find ourselves not only separated from God, but from everyone. It seems the way of the world is separation in which most living things seem like natural enemies. One animal preys upon another animal, people fight and argue amongst themselves, man separates from his wife, parents from their children, friend from friend, employers from employees, and the list goes on and on. The way of the world is separation; the way of love is oneness. The good of God flows to all who become part of this oneness. The most important ingredient of any satisfactory relationship is love.

When we are sad, lonely, and can't muster the energy to get out of bed in the morning, how are we supposed to go out into the world and show love? I would suggest small baby steps and begin by starting with you. Start by being patient with yourself and those that you pass or encounter on a day-to-day basis. Then change your mind-set by reading inspirational things, listening to inspiring music, and seeking after good things. Seek for quietness to enter your life, and in that quietness, ask God where you can best serve. If you have not characteristically smiled at someone before, smile at them now. There are a million people in the world who are alone and afraid. Ask yourself who you can call just to say you were thinking of them.

If you genuinely want to find yourself, lose yourself in love by reaching out to others. If you want to honor the memory of someone you lost, honor it by showing love in their name. The things you have been through may have given you a better understanding of what others need, so who better to try than you?

Love

"Let no one ever come to you without leaving better and happier. Be the living expression of God's kindness: kindness in your face, kindness in your eyes and kindness in your smile."
—Mother Teresa

How great it is man can know
When he is hungry the fruits of the field can feed him,
And when he is thirsty, rivers can quench his thirst.
Yet, how can he till the soil of his spirit and reap the
harvest for his soul?
It is to rise above sorrow by hungering for miracles and grace,
Which gives nourishment and the strength to finish the race?

Spirit
A Tool of Understanding

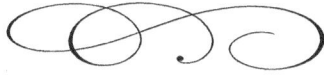

There is no life in the physical body unless there is a spirit present. This hit home more than ever when I began to spend a great deal of time in funeral homes. Time after time, I witnessed the distinct change in the physical body after the spirit left it. It was a change that was incomprehensibly yet consistently recognizable that transcended beyond the body just losing its life generating animation.

Every human that walks upon this earth has a spirit that has a physical form and agreed to experience the human condition for each individual purpose, one of which is to learn important lessons that are conducive to understanding love, compassion, and our individual value.

Even though I grew up in a Christ-centered home and believed I understood the principle of body and spirit, it didn't resonate with me because, like so many others, I didn't have a need to think about it—then, I lost someone I loved and my life and everything I desired changed. All of a sudden, I required more than an innocent faith. With every breath I took, an insatiable hunger to know more and more was born within me. I later came to recognize my hunger as that seed that dwells within each of us, and when we ask and seek to understand it, we receive the light that helps it grow into knowledge.

What exactly is a spirit? At my daughter's funeral, a brief and well-known example was given so that even the youngest members of the congregation could grasp the simplicity of it. The speaker held up has hand so that everyone could see it. "My hand," he said, "represents my spirit, that intangible part of me that God created. My spirit makes my body move, talk, and function." He then held up a white glove and proceeded to put the glove on the hand he was holding up until each sleeve of the glove snuggly covered each one of his fingers. "This glove represents my physical body," he went on as he one by one wiggled each finger. "This glove on its own cannot do much, and yet, when you combine it with a spirit, it is a wonderful sacred creation. The body can do so much in aiding the spirit to learn, to experience, and to comprehend many things, yet the body is not who I am, and it cannot stand alone."

Just like the glove, the spirit resembles the body; it takes on a similar form as the person it dwells in. Why is this important to know? Because you would recognize your loved one if you saw them. They are still real; they are still made of matter, even though it is a much finer matter, but matter nonetheless. If your physical eyes could see such fine matter, you would see them and you would recognize them. We are all spiritual beings and we are on earth to experience physical life.

What does the dictionary say about the meaning of body, spirit, or soul? The body means the material or physical structure of an organism; in this book, I am referring to mankind. However, every living thing was created spiritually before being placed on this earth. The body is the physical part of a person. The spirit by definition is of conscious life; the vital principle in humans, animating the body, or mediating between body and soul.

The spirit is the spark of light, the living force that is placed in your physical body by direction of our creator, God. We utilize our physical body until it dies and leaves the realm of this physical earth. The definition of soul is credited with the faculties of thought, our psyche, and our emotions and is often conceived as an immaterial entity. A simple explanation could be to say that a soul consists of a body and spirit united in a temporary mortal union. Imagine your life came to an end and you were greeted by your loved ones as you stood there in your spiritual form, do you suppose you would see other spirits? Our spiritual body with its spiritual eyes could see. We hear of many accounts from people who have seen their loved ones in spirit form. Do you suppose you could look at them and see their soul, their invisible inner emotional intelligence, the part that makes them who they are? I don't know, but why would we need to? Communication would be enlightened beyond our ability right now to imagine. However, they are who they are; they are the same person without the physical form that helped them navigate life here on the earth. Complete understanding of the difference between the spirit and the soul isn't required to glean the meaning from this book and the meaning is that we are more than our physical bodies. When we die, we still exist.

Journal:

September 7, 1982, was quite a profound day. The girls were at school, it was a warm breezy day, which was normal September weather. Bryan, who was nine months old, was sleeping soundly in his crib and I decided to take a long overdue nap. I was unusually exhausted for some reason, not sure why, so I didn't hesitate to grab the opportunity to take some down time to close my eyes. It didn't take me long to fall asleep because I had no recollection of lying there thinking about anything. My memory and mind however was crystal clear as to what took place during that nap. I was in a different kind of sleep, an unfamiliar kind, because as I lay there, I got this pressing feeling that the girls would soon be home and the baby was going to wake and need me. I felt an urgency to wake up. I repeatedly tried to open my eyes, but it was as if they were glued shut. I kept trying until my frustration prompted me to get up anyway—even if my eyes wouldn't open, but my body had the heaviness of concrete and I couldn't move. I began to feel anxious, then afraid. I remember wondering if I had died, but if I had, then death meant being aware, but stuck in darkness and helplessness. When my fear turned to panic, I suddenly opened my eyes. I lay there and looked around the room relieved that I could see, and I focused on the wall above the bedroom door and stared at the reflection of water dancing on it. I knew a breeze was tickling the water in our pool and a ray of light had sent it through the patio door where I could watch the soothing rhythm of it dancing on the wall as if it were trying to keep time to music. I looked over at the clock on the dresser and knew the girls wouldn't be home for at least another three hours, so there was no urgency to get up, what was I thinking? I looked back at the dancing water and it made me entertain the idea of swimming when they got home. I felt relaxed and peaceful as other thoughts paraded through my mind until I heard a sound that was foreign to me. It was a combination of chimes or metal on metal and the closest thing to describing it was as if someone was trying to put silverware away in a drawer. I became concerned and thought I should get up and check it out—maybe someone else was in the house. I tried to get up, but I couldn't move. I was awake, but still couldn't manage to move my body. I tried again to sit up, all the while watching the water dance on the wall, and after trying a couple more times, I finally managed to pull myself into a sitting position, only to notice that I was sitting but my body wasn't. However, I was content to just sit there; I had no sense of urgency about anything. I wasn't even alarmed that my body in a strange kind of way wasn't even connected to me. I continued to watch the water dance on the wall and occasionally turned my head to look out the window at the pool or around the room, but before long, my attention was loudly interrupted by a loud rumbling noise coming from the backyard (which I learned later was a garbage truck taking a shortcut through the alley behind our house) and the loud noise startled me enough to jerk me into physical consciousness and I realized I was no longer sitting, even though I never made the decision to lie back down. I lay there continuing to observe everything in the room like the reflection of the water, things on the dresser, and the digital clock, but realizing I had just physically awakened from my nap, yet I knew I had been awake long before that. I lay there for a while, overwhelmed by my experience, and yet at the same time feeling elated. I was in awe of the fact that I knew there was definitely more to me than my body. I actually had a personal witness that my spirit truly existed. My consciousness during the nap was as aware and real as anything I had ever experienced in the physical, but I did wonder why it had happened to me and why on that day. I couldn't help but speculate throughout the day that perhaps everyone at some point is given some kind of experience like that to kindle in their souls a desire to know more about who they really are.

Three days after my nap experience, I was standing at the bedside of my daughter in the intensive care unit at the hospital. I had just been told that with her severe head trauma, there was no way she could survive. I soon began to understand what had been given to me three days earlier. I knew that she would be aware of her surroundings when her spirit separated from her body. In the midst of my sorrow, I was comforted by knowing that and I believe it was nothing less than a wonderful gift I was given. It did confirm to me that life was more than the physical body we lay down when we die. It was something I wish everyone could know, but working with many others in grief, I knew many didn't experience anything remotely similar. I questioned for a long time, why me? Then I began to realize that many people do experience miracles and do receive spiritual messages, probably more than we know, but depending on their history of beliefs or what is going on in their lives at the time, just don't recognize or understand them. I also came to know that it is by pure grace we are given these miracles. We don't have to earn them or ask for them— sometimes, they just happen. On occasion, we are simply not aware of grace when it appears or we don't stop long enough to listen, and sometimes skepticism tries to convince us it is nothing. Even though my grief was consuming, I started to reflect back on the days before Lanette died and began recalling other messages that were gifted to me.

Journal:

It's been about four weeks since the funeral. Mom came back to spend more time with me and we have been talking about how strong Lanette's spirit is in our home. It feels peaceful with her here, and I have been thinking a lot about other things that happened before she died. I had to admit that I had been given other subtle messages that were no doubt provided to help me understand her leaving.

About a week before her death, Lanette quietly slipped into my room in the middle of the night and stood by my bed without saying a word, and even though I had been sleeping quite soundly, I awoke to feel the presence of one of my children. I think it's an inner sense given to mothers to know when their children need them. I would always wake when my kids came into my room no matter how tired I was. I tried to adjust my eyes in the dark to see who was standing there, but I finally reached

out and touched her leg and knew it was Lanette by the feel of her skin.
It seemed odd that it was her because she was always trying to show me
how independent she was. I asked what was wrong. "I don't know," she
said quietly, obviously confused herself why she had the need to come in
and be near me. My first initial reaction was the desire to tell her to go
back to bed, but a whisper powerful enough to silence me heard a com-
mand to "Get up!" I sat up and asked her if she was afraid, and again,
she said she didn't know. I went with her to her room and lay down be-
side her. I stroked her hair and rubbed her arms and told her that I loved
her and that I knew we didn't always see eye to eye on things, after all,
she was twelve and I was an adult, but I loved her more than she knew
and I was proud of the beautiful young lady she was becoming. We drift-
ed off to sleep in each other's arms, and I later realized that I was given
an opportunity to express my love for her and it was my only good-bye.

I was grateful I heard the command to get up and go back to her room
with her. I was thankful for that gift and realized how we don't tell people
often enough how much we love them. Sometimes, they leave us too soon
and we experience great regret.

It has taken me years to receive and fully acknowledge those gifts for
what they were. It is too easy to get caught up in the skepticism that blocks
our vision and we slip right off that slope of believing that whispers and
miracles are not what they seem because they are not announced with
trumpets. Sadly, we can spend our lives not allowing our hearts to receive
these transmitted spiritual messages. Getting our own life-limiting fear
out of the way and raising our antennae can definitely let in the light to lift
the fog of unbelieving. Getting out of our way can be hard, but possible.

Buddha once said: "Be a light unto yourself." When we are confronted
with situations that test us to the depths of our soul and we have nowhere
to run or hide, shifting our perspectives can help. Understanding the light
within yourselves to receive the things of the spirit can help you understand that you don't need to run and hide, but you need to understand
and comprehend what is available to you. We can let our light show us
how to take baby steps toward accepting and understanding. We can also

serve as mirrors for others without even realizing it. When we get it...we can teach it—the lessons of our life is to learn about our spirit, and when we learn, we also begin to know that we can share it. We are both students and teachers in this life. Someday, when a student is ready, you may be the teacher they need. So be a light to yourself, then one to others.

We have heard many times by today's spiritual leaders that we are all spiritual beings having a human experience and it is true. A characteristic of being spiritual is being advanced in awareness. Allowing spiritual consciousness is what we should aspire to achieve. Every day that we live, we have an opportunity to expand our consciousness and understanding, and by becoming aware of our thinking, it changes the choices we make each and every moment of our lives.

What stands the test of experience? It is Truth. It is the fulfillment of our spiritual destiny when we learn that through the true tests of experience we have gained far more and been compensated far more than anything the world considers lost. We are not lost, we never were. God created and knows each and every one of us. He created us spiritually and then sent us to school to learn.

Let thankfulness be the beginning of my gratitude.
Let it grow to its completion so that it may
Not only be in the words I speak,
But in the way I love and the way I act.
Let me be grateful for not only
Happiness and abundance,
But for divine grace, truth and life itself.

Gratitude
A Tool of Doing

I t might seem hard to believe that one of the simplest acts can pack the biggest punch when it comes to applying it in our lives. In fact, it might seem too simple to be effective. As a small child, were you admonished to say "thank you" for something someone gave you or did for you? Was it gratitude you felt when you were told to do it? Probably not, but many parents want to teach their children the value of not only feeling thanks, but expressing it as well. Most people claim that they are not mind readers, so if someone is thankful and they don't express it, how is the one giving to know? It is interesting to note that saying thank you isn't really for the person that did the kind deed as much as it is for the one on the receiving end. God doesn't want us to express gratitude to make him feel better; he wants us to express gratitude because he knows it is an important part of our soul's growth and the direct path to which we can know of his love.

Parents try to teach their children the concept of gratitude in small ways, but how much of it do they feel in their hearts on an everyday basis while small but countless blessings parade by in plain view? This is what God wants us to see!

There is great power and healing in gratitude. If you need another miracle in your life to lift you, try expressing gratitude for the ones, small or large, that you have already been given. If you don't know where to direct it, look up to the heavens and say, "Thank you." It can be as easy as that.

It's very easy to be grateful when things are going good or when we have just received a great unexpected gift. In fact, we may be so excited that gratitude becomes delight before we knew it was coming. Yet sometimes, we get so busy and caught up in our troubles that we don't consider the things that are going right or the blessings we already have, let alone expressing any kind of appreciation for them.

My mother used to tell me that when I felt like praying the least is when I should pray the most. That is how I feel about gratitude and appreciation. It is hard to feel grateful when life has knocked our feet out from under us, yet it is that time when we should seek and acknowledge our blessings the most.

The feelings of sincere appreciation are so much more than gratitude. It is actually an energy-producing force that can harness the light and love you need in your life to heal you faster than anything I know. Do you want another magic pill? Well, gratitude is one of them. The great thing is this energy can be tapped into by anyone.

Having an attitude of gratitude isn't going to make everything better instantaneously or persuade you to believe your pain is not real. It doesn't mean you have to be happy about what has transpired in your life to break your heart. Having gratitude doesn't mean you can't wish that things could have been different or that you can't try to change things the best way you can. You don't have to be blind to suffering or harmful situations either. Being grateful doesn't take away whatever life lessons will come from pain, it just tries to help you see that you are still alive and part of the world that is tending to you. We don't have a crystal ball to see into the future to know why things happen as they do and for what purpose. We can only hope that it is for a purpose greater than we may comprehend and until we can comprehend or appreciate the answers, grace just might have to carry us, but gratitude will help hold us up.

When you are suffering and you don't know where to begin to not only have your love of life restored to you, but the desire to want it, you need all the help and energy you can get to propel you forward, and small feelings or words of appreciation can align you with a that powerful source of energy capable of moving you out of energy resistance. When you are not energy resistant, you gradually move into the energy flow where you are more likely to receive further guidance and inspiration. Your heart's eye begins to see the help and support that is there for you.

Gratitude

Have you ever been around unhappy people who mumble that their life is so miserable that they have nothing to be grateful for, and yet you look at them and without batting an eye, count in your mind numerous things about them or their life that you instantly recognize as a blessing? I have tried to point out blessings to some people like that, but some choose to remain blind. Sometimes, the seed of gratitude has lain dormant in individuals for so long that you wonder if it was ever planted in the first place, but it was. If gratitude isn't sprouting in your life, it just may take a little more water and a little more tending to than it may for others, but the effect is just as powerful.

I have often told my children when they seem to be so unhappy about the way life is dealing with them that taking a moment to recognize the good things that they do have will inspire them to know what they need to focus on to create change. Many of us have been conditioned to believe that not being satisfied is the same as not being happy. A good way to approach this is to feel grateful and satisfied about the blessings in your life while still moving forward to achieving the ones you want. Wise stewardship over the blessings and things in your life is the best reason for God to bestow more upon you. If you can't handle a small blessing, what will you do with a large one?

It has been repeatedly proven that those things we focus on are the things we attract. If you focus on what you do not have, you will get more disappointments. If you focus on gratitude and love, wholeness and healing will draw closer to you. The law of resonance teaches us that the energy we put out is the energy we get back. There is no higher vibration than love, and gratitude is the first step in getting you to recognize, feel, and share in love. If you just uttered one prayer a day, let it be a prayer of thanks, for even then it would be enough, but go a step further and look around and appreciate other things no matter how small. Sincere gratitude can short-circuit negative feelings that can literally be harmful to your body, thereby zapping you of the much needed energy you need to heal. It is possible to feel peace even when you are sad or upset, yet gratitude can give you an assurance and feeling that this too will pass.

Expressing gratitude is not going to be an instant cure-all for your pain, nor is it going to guarantee you that you will never suffer again, but what it does give is a healing balm to your soul. If you speak it with sincerity or feel it in your heart, it will raise your energy vibration and can actually bring you to better physical health and spiritual happiness.

My daughter loved rainbows. We had sky-blue wallpaper with white clouds on her bedroom wall. We worked together the summer before she died to make her room a little bit of heaven. I taught her how to use the sewing machine, and she made little satin rainbow pillows that she hung from the ceiling. She was proud of her room and the fact that it was beautiful because of her creativity. So imagine the miracle of a beautiful rainbow right over the funeral home for two days as we held her viewing. I couldn't help but feel overwhelming gratitude for the tender miracle that God gave us on an otherwise sunny day in Arizona. It gave me the peace I needed to get through those impossible-to-bear first days. I was new to grief and couldn't know the trials that were to follow, but for that moment, I was grateful for the rainbow because it reminded me that it held a promise, and I needed to feel that promise. When difficult days followed, I tried to go back and think about the rainbow, and again, I felt grateful.

Someone once asked me if I knew that I would lose my child at such a young age and have to experience the pain of her loss, would I do it again if I had the choice? "I would do it in a heartbeat!" I said, "Absolutely!"

I have a million beautiful memories of funny, cute, trying, and beautiful things that I love about her to hold me over until I see her again. Yes, I wish she could have stayed longer, and yes, I wish I could have attended her graduation, her wedding, and the birth of her children, but live without knowing her, absolutely not. I am so grateful for her life and the time she had with me that my heart overflows when I think about it. I still see her face in my mind, I still hear her chuckle when she was being funny, and I even treasure the tears she cried when she was sad. I treasure her and I am and always will be grateful she came to earth as my daughter and that I was trusted with the job of taking care of her until she was called home. Those feelings give me strength. God had to love me to let me experience her.

Even in your pain, take a few moments to remember and share in all the good memories you have been given. I was once told by a wise man that one of the best things we can do for the people we love is to create good memories with them. Even the smallest of joyous times together can affect the gratitude center of the brain and be remembered for years to come. We remember things that affect our emotions.

When my children speak of their childhood, they do not recall the new toys they got for Christmas or when their allowance had been increased or decreased for that matter, but they remember trips to the orange orchard and coming home to make jam together, or they talk about going to the petting zoo and feeding the animals. Christmastime is seeing relatives and laughing and sharing. It was a time to sing together or make funny little skits to perform in front of the family. Sometimes, the kids and I would sit around and tell jokes and laugh so hard our sides would ache. When we have memories, they hold us over until we can be together again. What a wonderful gift we are given when we see the wisdom in memory and we recognize the power we have to create them. Start there with your gratitude. What memories do you have that can bring a smile to your face, a tear of joy to your eye, or a soothing relief to your soul? When you come up with even one, small or large, be grateful.

If we allow the healing spirit of God to help us deal with our grief, we become aware of many things that we wouldn't otherwise begin to be sensitive to. That is why a gratitude journal can be therapeutic because we can later go back when we need to remember that we were literally carried most of the time, and those memories can continue to serve in our healing and also be an inspiration to others who are going through their trials. With gratitude, we get closer to seeing the bigger picture, and when we have a glimpse of the bigger picture, we are experiencing the light.

Oh let me pray
When day has begun
So in my sorrow
I may see the sun.
Let your guidance
Be my light
So I may discern
Which path is right.
Let me know wisdom
That has no end.
But please, dear God
Let my prayers
Make you my friend.

Prayer
A Tool of Doing

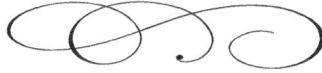

As a small child, I usually uttered a quick prayer before I jumped into bed. It was a routinely repetitive prayer without much thought of it being answered—but it was a beginning. I am sure that the words were not as important as the fact that at a young age, I was encouraged to open up a line of communication with God. Understanding the miraculous process of a simple childhood prayer came later as I began to grow in understanding of just how God related to my life, but as a child, I always felt safer when I would go to sleep after I prayed.

As I prayed for inspiration on how to present this chapter, I was continually urged to keep it simple. The Bible is full of scriptures on why we should pray and what the benefits of prayer are as we try to navigate the raging seas of our earthly mortality. One can study and read about prayer in many places and hear the testimonies from many people of the power that prayer has played in their lives, and it continually reaffirms that prayer should be a part of every life if we are to be able to tap into the greatness of this universe and our relationship with God.

I have no doubt that God loves us and desires our happiness. He has so much in store for us, but a good relationship requires good conversation, and when we pray, we deepen our relationship with him. The invitation to talk with God is for our benefit and our trust-filled dependence on him leads us to be able to ask for what we need. Every intimate relationship is a two-way street. Communication is crucial to intimacy. Prayer is talking to God, thereby, creating intimacy with him.

It is easy to pray and give thanks when we feel blessed and things are going great. But one of the greatest tests of courage is to pray when trials and tribulations seem to rob us of our faith and our ability to feel gratitude. How sad to live our lives without stopping for a moment and recognize the fact that God loves us and wants us to ask for guidance and comfort when we need it.

When I found myself single again, I decided to take up dancing, and I met a man at a church dance who seemed to share the same interest, so for six years, we met on Saturday evenings to dance. Occasionally, we would meet up to take short trips to the coast or take a day or two to go see a beautiful natural attraction in our state. He loved history and would map out all the historical places he wanted to visit during his lifetime and many times asked me to go with him. When we would visit beautiful places that I probably would not have visited if he hadn't invited me and looking at them through his eyes, I developed a greater love for nature and appreciation for him. We both knew that the relationship wouldn't progress to more than friendship, and I knew eventually he would seek one that would, but for the time we shared, it was therapeutic for us both to have someone to talk to. Yet when the time came and he moved on, I was confused at the amount of pain I felt. I felt abandoned. What eventually became clear to me over time was that I missed our conversations. We both participated in our talks, which usually took place in the mornings because he worked at night. In the beginning, I didn't think I had the time to engage in his casual light-hearted conversation, but I grew to look forward to them. During those six years, we discussed everything under the sun and I became acquainted with him on a personal level. I listened as he talked about his children, his beliefs, and the wounds he carried from his childhood. As I listened, I began to open up, and when I did, I learned things about myself—it was therapeutic. When his calls stopped, I felt cut off from someone I learned to care for. I felt I knew him, and from knowing him, I appreciated him. I also appreciated him for not only getting me to talk but also in listening to me. The silence was very loud for a while.

When you are in a relationship with someone that doesn't want to talk or doesn't want to share, the silence can be difficult to endure. It is hard to get to know someone when they won't talk to you. In relationships, if someone cannot open up and risk vulnerability, how can you to get close to them? Silence in relationships can be the undoing of that relationship.

Prayer

Prayer, like conversation, is no respecter of persons: it does not care whether you are rich or poor, sad or happy, wise or ignorant, or what religion you are; it isn't only about asking for help or inspiration, but more about opening up a conversation with God about your life.

God created each one of us with a longing for intimacy— intimacy with him and intimacy in our relationships. Intimacy is nourished with conversation. If we come to the understanding of what he is asking when he asks us to talk to him, we can come to the realization that we were created to fellowship him and walk with him. We need him and he desires us. The more we walk and talk with him, the more time we spend with him, the more our eyes will see every shade of his personality. Can you imagine taking a walk along a beautiful garden path with someone you know and trust, someone you know loves you and has compassion for you, someone that can help you understand what you need to do when you are faced with a challenge? No matter how many times we ask him to take a walk with us, he will not push us away; he will only draw us closer. The kind of prayer that is generated with intimacy is the powerful kind that can move mountains and produce miracles. True intimacy happens when it is coupled with a willingness to be known by him. Even though we know God knows everything, it is when we take down our guard and desire to get honest about our fears that we begin to learn about ourselves. Being alone with God, whether it be on that garden path, a dark quiet room, or standing at the edge of the sea is when we experience the reward of intimacy, friendship and safety. Imagine it, the living God, the God of the universe, wants to live in friendship with us. He wants a relationship of trust, and he knows it needs to be nurtured through prayer. In the New Testament, the story of Jesus calming the sea is a good example of being able to ask for help. It starts after Jesus finishes teaching the multitude of people on the shore some parables, then he turns to his disciples and tells them it is time to get in the boat and cross to the other side.

And the same day, when the even was come, he saith unto them, Let us pass over unto the other side. And when they had sent away the multitude, they took him even as he was in the ship. And there were also with him other little ships. And

there arose a great storm of wind, and the waves beat into the ship, so that it was now full. And he was in the hinder part of the ship, asleep on a pillow: and they awake him, and say unto him, Master, carest thou not that we perish? And he arose, and rebuked the wind, and said unto the sea, "Peace, be still". And the wind ceased, and there was a great calm. And he said unto them, why are ye so fearful? How is it that ye have no faith? And they feared exceedingly, and said one to another, What manner of man is this, that even the wind and the sea obey him?
Mark 4:35-41 (kjv)

Their boat is being tossed around in a violent storm, and the whole time, Jesus is asleep. How many times in our lives have we asked the same question: Is Jesus asleep in our lives? Is God asleep in our lives? Haven't we all experienced those feelings that God seems to be asleep at the wheel? Of course, Jesus cared about his disciples on the boat, but what took them so long to wake him and ask for help? In his wisdom and for the sake of them, he waited until they asked for his help. He wanted them to make him more completely a part of their lives. The disciples could have woken him much sooner and he would have gladly calmed the sea. He would not have been bothered by them. As with Jesus, God wants to be bothered. He wants us to have conversations with him. Yes, we should go to him when major storms come into our lives, but we should also seek him out when things are okay so that we may grow in our understanding of him and friendship with him.

When I have had a conversation with God and I go about my daily activities, it seems that I am more protected with his umbrella of influence. I seem to be more aware of my surroundings and more peaceful as I go about my day. Sometimes, I feel that he is just walking silently beside me, there if I need him, and quiet when I need to figure a few things out on my own. It's more difficult to open up a conversation when I have allowed too much time to pass without talking to him. I get embarrassed and sometimes feel guilty, but I need to let go of those feelings because I know that when I speak, he listens, and it is I that experiences the comfort and peace when I do call in. I think he just smiles knowing that it took me a while—but I called.

Prayer

So what do we do when our boat is tossing about in the sea or we are alone in the wilderness? Where do we begin our journey back? If we are not used to asking for help or we feel too detached because up to this point we have made it on our own, how do we find the strength to cast our burdens upon God's shoulders?

Think about this for a moment: George Washington, the first president of the United States, recognized the hand of God on occasions during the country's early battles to establish independence. On November 3, 1789, he wrote in a letter: "The success, which has hitherto attended our united efforts, we owe to the gracious interposition of Heaven; and to the inter-position let us gratefully ascribe the praise of victory, and the blessings of peace."

One of the most famous paintings of George Washington depicts him on his knees at Valley Forge during the winter of 1777 when the colonial forces were almost defeated by the cold winter, shortages of clothing, food, and military supplies. One of the greatest adversaries, however, was that of discouragement.

Mason L. Weems, a biographer of Washington, wrote:

"In the winter of "77", while Washington, with the American army lay encamped at Valley Forge, a certain good old Friend (Quaker), of the respectable family and name of Potts, if I mistake not, had occasion to pass through the woods near head-quarters. Treading his way along the venerable grove, suddenly he heard the sound of a human voice, which as he advanced increased on his ear, and at length became like the voice of one speaking much in earnest. As he approached the spot with a cautious step, whom should he behold, in a dark natural bower of ancient oaks, but the commander in chief of the American armies on his knees at prayer! Motionless with surprise, friend Potts continued on the place till the general, having ended his devotions, arose, and, with a countenance of angel serenity, retired to head-quarters: friend Potts then went home, and on entering his parlor called out to his wife, 'Sarah, my dear! Sarah! All's well! All's well! George Washington will yet prevail!'

"'What's the matter, Isaac?' replied she; 'thee seems moved.'

"'Well, if I seemed moved, 'tis no more than what I am. I have this day seen what I never expected. Thee knows that I always thought the sword and the gospel utterly inconsistent; and that no man could be a soldier and a Christian at the same time. But George Washington has this day convinced me of my mistake.'

"He then related what he had seen, and concluded with the prophetical remark—"If George Washington be not a man of God, I am greatly deceived—and still more shall I be deceived if God does not, through him, work out a great salvation for America. 4

President Abraham Lincoln sought out God when he needed divine guidance. When General Stickles noticed that before the battle of Gettysburg, President Lincoln appeared free from the overwhelming care that frequently weighed him down. After the battle, he asks Lincoln how it was that he seemed at peace when surely he knew that the fate of the nation hung on that battle.

Lincoln said, "Well, I will tell you how it was. In the pinch of your campaign up there, when everybody seemed panic- stricken and nobody would tell what was going to happen, oppressed by the gravity of our affairs, I went to my room one day and locked the door and got down on my knees before Almighty God and prayed to Him mightily for victory at Gettysburg. I told Him that this war was His and our cause His cause, but we could not stand another Fredericksburg or Chancellorsville. Then and there I made a solemn vow to Almighty God that if he would stand by our boys at Gettysburg, I would stand by Him, and he did stand by you boys, and I will stand by Him. And after that, I don't know how it was, and I cannot explain it, soon a sweet comfort crept into my soul. The feeling came that God had taken the whole business into His own hands, and that things would go right at Gettysburg, and that is why I had no fears about you."5

Prayer

It is out of the depths of true prayer that an individual, whether he is a great leader or a faithful follower, can raise to great heights. If we have been inspired to ask God to provide safety and comfort, would it not stand to reason that he is waiting and he does have the power to intervene and make a difference? Many studies have claimed that prayer can relieve stress, improve attitudes, and mend our bodies. Sincere prayer generates peace, power, and good health. It can even prevent anxiety and disease. Prayer is a simple act that has been proven time and time again capable of healing. Prayer enhances the mind-body-soul connection.

If you haven't prayed much in your life and you are not sure how to go about it, it is very easy, just do it. Lift your eyes to the heavens and tell God you need him to teach you. He will because God reveals himself to us through prayer. Thank him that we don't have to understand prayer in order to pray. When we pray, God is helping us to grow. We don't pray to impress him or inform him because we can't tell God anything that he doesn't already know. We pray to invite him into our lives, and through our prayers, he helps us grow.

Have you ever prayed and didn't immediately get the answer you were looking for? Did you keep praying but also began to search your heart and life to see if you were hindering God's answer? Many times, we are the ones stopping the answer, yet when we figure it out, aren't we stronger?

I try not to pray with a grocery list of wants or a way to get God to change his mind, but as a way of discerning his will. Sometimes, I just can't seem to figure things out on my own. I ask for his presence when I need to be strong, and I ask for understanding. I also find myself asking for inspiration, because I have learned that if I stop and listen he will send a clear strong message, sometimes so strong that I can't help but jump in jubilation for the wonderful gift.

A faith-promoting story of my own came quietly and powerfully when I had fallen and hurt my knee a few years ago. I had no health insurance and time managed to inflame the injury until I could barely walk. I visited the emergency room a couple of times, and without insurance, I was sent home with medication that eventually had no effect on my pain. I was trying to take care of my elderly father and I also had guardianship of my grandson and I was sorely falling short of my responsibilities. Conversations with God at the time were few and far between; even then, I felt there wasn't much he could do with my kind of pain. How I could feel that way when I had personally witnessed many miracles, I don't know, but I guess my humanness and stubbornness made me pull away. I contacted an orthopedic surgeon to see if there was anything he could do that wouldn't require surgery or hospitalization. An MRI alone was about twenty-five hundred dollars. The doctor understood and said he was pretty sure what the problem was, so we could bypass the MRI, and he'd take payments for his fees, but the hospital was going to require full payment up front, and that was more than I had. I didn't know what to do! I was completely immobilized because lying in bed was painful, but standing was as well. I was still taking pain medication, but it only made me feel numb. About a year after the accident, I was lying in bed feeling totally hopeless, and in the middle of the night, I desperately said a prayer asking God to help me deal with the pain. I no sooner got the words out when I felt a snap in my knee and the pain stopped. The first thing I wanted to do was rationalize what happened, but I stopped because I knew what God was capable of. I knew from the depths of my soul, so why did I need to validate it? Again, it was the human part of me, but this time, I was going to take it and run with it. A thought told me my true test of faith would come in the morning when I got out of bed and walked down the stairs. I believed I would handle the stairs without difficulty or pain, and I wasn't going to take any medication to do it. I also received the message that my knee, the meniscus cartilage, was still torn and that I was to seek help to repair it, but I would be out of pain until I could find it. The fact that I was out of pain seemed like enough of a miracle, but it didn't end there. About a week later, a letter arrived informing me that I had been approved for free medical help from the Samaritan Health Services, and my prior emergency room bills and services for the following year would be taken care of. If I had ever held a miracle in my hands, it was that letter. I was nervous about visiting the new doctor I was referred to because I wasn't in pain and I was afraid he would send me home and say, "Well, since there is no pain, there is no need to have surgery." But instead, he came in and told me it was his usual practice to ask his patients if he could have a word of prayer with them so that God would lead him to understand how to best serve their needs. He also said he always prayed before he performed surgery so God would steady and guide his hands. I guess from the look on my face and the way my eyes widened, he drew back and said he didn't mean to offend me. He realized that some people were not into prayer, but he always asked anyway. Tears welled in my eyes as I told him that he didn't know how afraid I had been to come in and tell him that even though I wasn't in pain, I still had an injury that God told me needed to be taken care of. We bowed our heads and he offered a prayer, and then, we scheduled the surgery. I went home that day with my heart so full of gratitude that I could barely function. A week later, surgery was performed, and when I came out of the anesthetic, the doctor showed me a picture of my injury taken while they had my knee open. He told me in all of his years of practice he had never seen a meniscus cartilage torn so bad. After rehabilitation, exercise and extreme gratitude, I walk just fine. I can't imagine what I would have done had I not asked God to get me through that storm.

Many years ago, representatives from leading nations of the world met in San Francisco to pen a constitution that would unify all nations. The chapter was near completion when one of the smaller nations suggested that they pray and insert the name of God and appeal to him for guidance. The proposal was voted down. Eventually, the United Nations Committee sensed the absence of something from that charter, and again, the prayer proposal was introduced. No one wanted to offend the atheists so they decided to compromise. They agreed that the best way to handle it was before each meeting, they would offer a moment of silence and each person could bow his head in silence and pray as he desired.

Compare this to Benjamin Franklin and the other originators of the Constitution of the United States. They also started without prayer until finally Benjamin Franklin arose and said: "I have lived, Sir, a long time; and the longer I live, the more convincing proofs I see of this truth; that God governs in the affairs of men. And, if a sparrow cannot fall to the ground without his notice, is it probable that an empire can rise without his aid? We have been assured, Sir, in the Sacred Writings, that 'except the Lord build the house, they labor in vain that build it.' I firmly believe this; and I also believe, that, without His concurring aid, we shall succeed in this political building no better than the builders of Babel; we shall be divided by our little, partial, local interest, our projects will be confounded, and we ourselves shall become a reproach and a by-word down to future ages. And, what is worse, mankind may hereafter, from this unfortunate instance, despair of establishing government by human wisdom and leave it to chance, war, and conquest. "I therefore beg leave to move, That henceforth prayers, imploring the assistance of Heaven, and its blessings on our deliberations, be held in this assembly every morning before we proceed to business; and that one or more of the clergy of this city be requested to officiate in that service." 6

If wisdom must come through effort, would it be right to assume that every great thing will require part of our physical abilities, intellectual abilities and soul power? When we are admonished to ask so that we can receive, then it is through prayer that we ask; remember as well that we must knock and we must seek.

I often wonder if most people really understand what the power of prayer holds or if they realize what a great gift it is to know that we can call on the powers of heaven to bless our lives in so many ways. We can ask for healing to our bodies, peace, and comfort or for guidance out of our personal wilderness and for the whisper that witness's truth to our souls.

If great and influential men have prayed for divine guidance,I deem it is also very important for each and every one of us to pray on behalf of our leaders so they may listen to the wisdom of God, and when we vote for someone, ask if this leader is a man of God. In the midst of so many world problems, we may find ourselves asking what we can each do to make this world a better place, and I am convinced it is by beginning with sincere prayer that we will know the answer.

It is our responsibility to seek knowledge and to make every effort to help ourselves and those we love, but there are times when we get stuck, and asking for help is okay; however, God doesn't expect our boat to fill with water before we do.

Music is the voice that calls attention to the soul,
It lends wisdom that can make a heart whole.
Music expresses that, which cannot be spoken,
Never silenced, untouched, or broken.
It is a language of love, or a port in the storm,
Its divinity designed to keep a spirit warm.
Music for the soul, never a lesson is for naught,
For within the spirit of harmony,
Some of life's splendid courses are divinely taught.

Music
A Hands on Tool

I f grief were an illness that could be addressed by magically reaching into a little black bag to pull out a drug capable of soothing you, giving you a sense of well-being, and inspiring gratitude in your heart, you would probably call that a miracle drug, wouldn't you? However, the supreme drug would have to be something that didn't come with a myriad of scary side effects as most of them do. I'm sure you've heard wonder drugs advertised, but they also breeze over the side effects with such speed that your conscious mind can't cautiously take notes. Yet they can mask symptoms of all kinds of troublesome conditions. However, in risking it, you have to be willing to trade one problem for possibly one or more new ones. Maybe it's not such a miracle if it just seems safer to deal with your ailment instead of trying to mask the symptoms with a new drug. The miraculous medicine then would have to be one that when prescribed would only have safe positive side effects and pleasurable results.

Grief, though, is not an illness, it is a natural condition and it is well recognized that the death of a loved one, diagnosis of terminal illness, divorce, or other life-altering events can trigger deep clinical depression if not recognized for the serious stressor that it can be. If it is not addressed or grief is interrupted, it can remain unfinished business or morph into something more complicated and longer lasting. It's hard to imagine that grief is a natural condition when it seems to have such painful and sometimes hopeless feelings associated with it. Antidepressants or mood-altering drugs will not heal grief; some may interrupt it, but in the end, a larger wound will be there waiting—and screaming for attention.

There is that famous saying that we've probably heard a few times: "Time heals all wounds," but left on its own without work, it is less healing than the adage suggests. Besides, what do you do until time does its thing? That is where the miraculous medicine in the little black bag comes in and helps healing begin—music, it is an amazing miraculous wonder drug.

When time has passed and you have worked your way through some of your grief, you will see that in some respects, time can help, but probably not in the ways you wish it would. Time alone does nothing if it is not used wisely. Grief can build you into steel where you were once weak or crack you like a twig if you ignore it, but it will not stand idly by if you leave it alone. It will twiddle away each day, subtly hindering your healing.

If there was ever a time you needed a miracle medicine to help you, grief is certainly one of those times. We are given many gifts or "miraculous medicines" to help us, but we have to recognize and use them in order for them to work. Recognizing the gift of music and the immense power it holds is the first step to accepting it and letting its healing powers be part of your therapy. Sounds have the potential to touch your spirit and create thoughts that inspire you to attract that which you desire.

Pause for a moment and think about the creation of the universe. Everything was created within the harmony of natural law. All matter is organized to work in harmony with life. We are governed by laws—physical ones, spiritual ones, universal ones, and all of these laws complement each other. Energy is organized and fits into the mathematical harmony of cause and effect. It, much like math, has tones that are created in patterns that can affect our minds and emotions in either good ways or, if created outside the patterns of good sounding harmony, in negative ways. Music has healing properties when it is harmonious, and healing takes place when the music is soothing, but when it sounds conflicting, it can actually cause illness. Every law has a positive or a negative force behind it, yet all are created to fulfill a purpose, and when we reach out to the gifts of them all, we have access to more powers and awareness than we can even begin to comprehend. Every sound is a vibration of powerful energy. The earth and the universe move together in perfect harmony. Watch the breeze gently move the tree and you can see rhythm. Think of a song that has always moved you to emotion and play it in your mind as you watch the wave's crash on the shore—observe how they move with the music. Go out into nature and listen—it all has music. Stand by a babbling brook, water rushing downstream, grass rustling in a breeze, birds singing, and rain dancing on a window—all music.

Our world without music would be inconceivable. Music has been with us from the beginning and the transformative power of music has been recognized throughout history in all cultures and all people because everything was created with and for harmony. We began in the womb with rhythm and harmony by experiencing the heartbeat of our mother and tuning in to the sound of her voice. As infants we were soothed by being rhythmically rocked and sung to. As toddlers, our chants became nursery rhymes and learning to count by singing our numbers- one two buckle my shoe and so forth. Music is primal to life and harmony is instilled in us—in our language, our movements and our spirits. Yet it can be expressed in many different ways whether it be tapping our toes to the rhythm of a song, beating a drum, or remembering a special time or a melody that stirred memories of the past. Music is limitless in its ability to transform the participant to a heightened state of awareness. It has been believed by many that medicine heals the body and music heals the soul. This speaks truth when you realize that all healing first takes place from within. Our spirits begin the healing for the physical. Music has the ability to bypass the walls and barriers of our minds and physical bodies and go straight to the soul. Soft beautiful music is like a beautiful white light and it is pure. It links the heart of the listener with the heart of the creator. It can act as a spirit guide in some ways by transporting you into another world—a world of awareness. The spiritual world is so much more aware than the physical world. Music can transport you beyond your normal five senses.

We have talked about being a multi-sensory person, and music is like the electronic tuner that tunes you into other wavelengths, much like tuning your radio to another station. If you are spiritually tuned in and you are supposed to receive the message, you will receive it. I compare it to a large zipper that runs the length of my body, and when I need to understand something, music unzips the zipper and allows the message to harmonically flow right to my heart.

What kind of music tunes us in to these wonderful spiritual benefits? There are many kinds, so how do we choose the kind that can promote healing and comfort because music also has the ability to resist healing and good feelings. The goodness of your soul will fight against music that is meant to have negative responses. My truth meter will ask, "Does it make me feel good? Am I inspired to be giving? Do I want to be loving and positive?" If you listen to music that inspires rebellion or destructive behavior, you will know that it is not inspired to heal, teach, or promote love. Is it beautiful or is it ugly, does it lift you up or drag you down? God gives us the sense to know the difference as he does with other things in our lives. Does peace come over you or agitation? We always have the choice.

If you can't tell right away, listen a moment longer to see if it grows flowers or weeds. Just like Jesus admonished us about the tares and the wheat, the reason was to let it grow until the harvest so we could tell the difference. He said by their fruits, we would know them.

So if you want to know the differences between good fruits or bad, good literature or bad, good food or bad food, good music or bad music, you can tell just by how it makes you feel. Do you feel good?

Good music is to inspire you to draw closer toward emotional balance and to receive and hear the gifts of the spirit. It should make us desire to be friendly and happy. Good music will inspire you and cause you to want to move to action like giving acts of love, kindness, mercy, and compassion. At the right moment, positive music can make you feel like dancing or feel like laughing. It can be as simple as a few harmonic chords played gently on a piano or a violin softly moving air through the strings. It can be a song that you associate with, someone you care for, or a wonderful memory. It doesn't have to be a symphony or an orchestra with several different instruments, even though some are beautiful and very inspiring, to touch your soul.

It never ceases to amaze me how God thought of everything and how we live with these blessings right at our fingertips and many of us don't use them.

I was blessed to have piano lessons when I was young and a mother who encouraged music to be a part of my life. I fought practicing, but the lessons were never wasted. Any kind of introduction or enjoyment of music is never for naught, and it is never too late to make it a part of your life. We are listeners, we are singers, we are dancers, we are composers, we are teachers, we are healers, etc. We are channels of harmony; how we use it, how we enjoy it, and how it moves us all is determined by what we want.

When I hear a marching band in a parade, tears well in my eyes and it inspires my patriotism and my courage. When I hear a lullaby, it inspires my tenderness and my compassion. When I hear a ballad, it inspires my understanding, and when I sing,it inspires my creativity and my passion. I could go on and on as I sing the praises of music and try to inspire you to see the awesome magnificent gift it is.

We hear stories of great composers and wonder how some of them were given the gift to write symphonies at such a young age. Someone had to aide God in bringing it forth to us, and I believe the value of music was so great a necessity in our lives that God anointed some before they came to earth with the express purpose of bringing us the gift. I believe he blessed them to understand the patterns and principles of building music before they were even old enough to read.

Music theorist will use mathematics to understand the building of music. The basis of sound exhibits a range of number properties, simply because nature itself is astonishingly mathematical. Ancient Chinese and Egyptians were known to study the mathematical principles of sound, and the Pythagoreans of ancient Greece were the first researchers known to investigate the expression of musical scales in terms of numerical ratios of small numbers. Their belief was that all nature consists of harmony arising out of numbers.

From the time of Plato, harmony was considered an essential part of physics, now known as musical acoustics. Many studies stemming back to the early Indian and Chinese theorists show similar theories that mathematical laws of harmony and rhythm are fundamental to our understanding of not only the world but to the well-being of humans. Confucius regarded the small numbers 1,2,3,4, as the source of all perfection.

I wasn't aware of those things when I listened to music. I only knew how it affected me. I am sure Mozart didn't know it when he began showing his musical talents at three years old or at five when he learned his first musical piece or when he wrote his first composition. He was eight years old when he wrote his first symphony. He believed his ability to understand music wasn't because of a lofty degree of intelligence or imagination but it originated out of love. What is love? God is love.

Ludwig van Beethoven said: "Music is a higher revelation than all wisdom and philosophy. Music is the electrical soil in which the spirit lives, thinks and invents." Singer and songwriter John Denver said that music brings people together. It allows us to experience the same emotions because we are all the same in heart and spirit. It doesn't matter what language we speak or the color of our skin, music proves we are the same.

"A person does not hear sound only through the ears; he hears sound through every pore of his body. It permeates the entire being and according to its particular influence either slows or quickens the rhythm of the blood circulation; it either wakens or soothes the nervous system. It arouses a person to greater passions or it calms him by bringing him peace. According to the sound of its influence a certain effect is produced. Sound becomes visible in the form of radiance. This shows that the same energy which goes into the form of sound before being visible is absorbed by the physical body. In that way the physical body recuperates and becomes charged with new magnetism."7
—Hazrat Inayat Khan

Leonardo da Vinci says that our soul is composed of harmony and Plato claims that music gives soul to the universe and wings to our imagination. Thomas Carlyle says that music is the speech of angels and brings us near to the infinite while Victor Hugo says music expresses those things that cannot be said and makes some things impossible to be silent.

Music

We have been blessed with creative and inspired people so that we may enjoy their gifts. I am grateful for them because I have personally witnessed music's ability to heal.

How can you tap into the miracle in the little black bag so you may see for yourself how it can help you in your time of need and in your desire to see, understand, and feel the things your eye cannot see? Start listening to good music.

Journal:

> *I cannot explain the peace I am feeling today and have for this past month. It is as if Christ was walking the halls of my home and I feel his peace. I have been listening to heavenly music and it has been drawing me closer to Lanette more than I could have ever imagined possible. "O That I Were An Angel" has been music to my soul. Why didn't I know about that song before? Beautiful music has made me recall the story about the footprints in the sand, and I humbly have to admit that I am being carried these days all the time. I thought I knew so much before, but compared to how I seem to be able to connect with heaven now, I was just an infant in my knowledge. I believe music has been an instrument in opening the windows for me to see. How grateful I am!*

It is important to have supportive family and friends around especially in your time of grief, but they can't be with you every minute and you will have times when you need to be alone or when they just aren't available for whatever reasons. The thing about grief is the pain doesn't take a weekend off or say good night and let you get on with your sleep. It follows like an ever- faithful friend or body part. It is during those moments of being left with only yourself and your grief that music can be a perfect companion. Much like a friend, it can provide company the minute it is heard, yet it can stay with you for as long as you need it. While with you, you can carry on whatever activity you want to do, or you can sit quietly and it doesn't require you to speak or say anything. You can sing with it, sway with it, and even cry with it and it will not critic you or ask you to stop or interfere with the emotions you are feeling. It doesn't take the place of human companionship, but it can be put up there right along with it because it can do many things that a close friend can do and in some areas more.

Music in general can be a powerful ingredient for general daily good health for everyone. It can slow down brain waves to allow for other benefits to occur. It can reduce anxiety and tension. It can boost our immune system and regulate our heartbeat. It has positive effects on our respiratory system, our digestive system, and it helps ease stress and depression, and if you haven't already found out, depression tries to hitch a ride with grief.

One of the most important lessons I've learned about music is how it can stabilize my mind. When I listen to music that isn't loud or intrusive, I began to feel centered and relaxed. It doesn't always happen immediately, but when I began to feel relaxed and uplifted, I began to feel a distinct connection with my spirit. It is usually during those times that I can understand the meaning of things I read or feel the closeness of the spirit world, which is closer than most imagine. While in the peace of music, I can feel the presence of my child when I needed to talk to her or ask my mother a question or talk to God about what is on my mind. It's not always easy to connect with your inner consciousness that craves spiritual connection when this world is so busy and loud. We manage to have so many irons in the fire that finding a time to be quiet and alone can be a challenge, but your grief and good health depends on you to do it. Give your healing some of your precious quiet time and some of your much needed attention, and if you do, you will start to understand that you can become well in spite of your pain.

Find a place where you can be alone and listen. Sit in a favorite chair, lie on a soft bed, or a soft patch of grass. Build yourself a musical first aid kit by gathering soothing music, whether it is recorded soundscapes, simple piano music, or some of your favorite hymns—prepare so you can begin. In the beginning, until you know what it is that brings you to the place you want to be, avoid music that has loud drums or uncomfortable repetitive instruments that could be distracting. Then, close your eyes and listen. Don't try to force yourself to think of anything particular, just let it flow. This is a good time to let your mind wander while the music plays. Soak in the musical emotions. Expect nothing… just relax, just listen, and just breathe. If you are relaxed, you won't feel your body—you will float. It might take a few times to feel like you are actually being carried away with the harmony or the rhythms, especially if this is new to you, but don't give up. With a heart that is desirous of connecting, you will be able to connect. Emotions arise when listening to music, and if crying or sobbing follows, allow it, tears can be therapeutic.

Loved ones that have passed away are around more than we know, and they are in a place where they know the wisdom of being able to navigate this life without all the answers, but they are also desirous to reach out and let us know they are okay. We put up our walls and barriers that they can't get past. Sometimes, our pain and grief is so strong that the world could blow up around us and we wouldn't know it because we have become handicapped in our awareness. When we take the time to be still and let music help us relax and move into our spiritual world, we can begin to touch and feel the other side so much easier. You will know when your loved one is close. That is when it is possible to communicate with them and understand that they are okay.

If you aren't grieving for the loss of someone, but need help trying to figure a few things out or get past some hurtful experience, give music a chance to mellow you and you will be amazed at its power.

I remember a drizzly cloudy day in August a few years ago when I had just finished attending a beautiful musical presentation given by Michael Ballam at Brigham Young University. It was a touching performance, and when over, I was inspired to seek a serene spot on a patch of grass outside to just sit and reflect. The sun had come out and a cool breeze pushed the hot humid air aside to embrace me. The music had put me into a very grateful frame of mind, and with the embrace of the breeze, I looked up and noticed a beautiful rainbow right above me. I became aware of my daughter's presence telling me that she was okay and very much aware of her family. I couldn't remember ever feeling as close to her as I did that day. I sat there for a long time feeling euphoric because without a doubt she let me see her happiness, and I knew she was all right; we were going to be okay. It felt so good to know that.

Music is accepting and nonjudgmental; it doesn't ask more of you than you can give. When you don't know what to speak or how to feel, music can speak what you can't and lead you to feel what you can't see. We are all created to be the recipients of it. Embrace it, use it to help you travel those unknown roads, climb those mountains, and seek serenity and peace. And by the way, dance too.

If you want to quote God, do so by serving.
If your light goes out, rekindle it by serving.
If you are adrift at sea, let service be your compass.
If you are down, rise by serving.
If your journey is long, go the extra mile by serving.
If you are weary, help the tired by serving.
If you want to understand love, you will, by serving.

Service
A Miracle Tool

I f I could return home to the tranquil mooring of the harbor or turn back the hands of time, I would pray that I wouldn't forget what I have learned about the power and healing of service. Back then, life seemed simple. I had ordinary everyday routines and ordinary family activities and ordinary bumps in the road, which never seemed too insurmountable—being ordinary was comfortable. Most of us are creatures of habit. We like stability and predictability.

Many of us aren't willing to venture into uncharted seas if we are comfortably treading still waters. Complacency provided me with a false sense of knowing what life had in store for me. As John Lennon once said, "Living is easy with eyes closed." When things shifted, however, it was like being tossed out of kindergarten and hurled directly to Earth College 101. Most of us are blindsided by the shift and unprepared, yet the tough truth is: we can't turn back the hands of time! We can't undo what has happened even though we wish we could by spending countless hours thinking of all the "if onlys" and the "why me's" until we slam into gridlock and have to make a choice to move forward or stay stuck. Acceptance of what has happened is the first step to overcoming gridlock, so we can choose a path that nudges us forward toward healing. Service is the one path that propels you forward faster than anyone I know. Even Jesus said that whoever would lose his life for His sake would save it.

I grew up with the teaching that when you lost yourself in service, you would find yourself. I couldn't relate to that. I didn't know what feeling lost meant until I found myself grieving, but even then, the word lost didn't give validity to my heartache— certainly there had to be a better word to describe lost. I was in plain view—I wasn't lost, I was more adrift

141

than anything, but I was sure my survival was in danger. I used to hear that God never gave us more than we were able to handle, and my reply was, "Are you kidding? Yes, he does!"

Here is what I discovered about service: When I was involved in it, I wasn't dwelling so much on my pain, and when I truly desired to help someone, there was always a lesson or a gift I came away with. I didn't appreciate the meaning of lost until I recognized the meaning of found.

When I took care of my mother who was dying of cancer, I came away with knowledge on how I would deal with my own health issues one day. Sitting in the hospital while she slept, I began reading a book someone had given her on healing cancer and other illnesses with nutrition and other natural remedies. I asked her why she had not heeded the advice in the book and she said the information came too late for her, but she hoped I would study the book in case I should ever need to make a lifesaving decision, then I would be armed with the information. The day did arrive when I needed to make decisions about my health, and I believe I knew enough to make the right one for me. If I hadn't taken the time to sit by her side, then I would not have been familiar with that knowledge, and I would have also missed out on the closeness we shared.

Not long after my daughter's death, I was wrestling with how we were going to pay for the funeral and take care of the bills that were piling up. The insurance was not forthcoming and I was becoming concerned. While driving to the store one day, I was listening to the news and heard that a five-year-old girl who lived close by had been struck by a car in front of her home and died instantly. The news saddened me because I knew another family was beginning the same journey I was on. I felt this urge to go visit them—maybe they needed someone to be there who understood. I repeatedly tried to talk myself out of it by asking who I thought I was to intrude on their privacy. Yet the feeling wouldn't leave me until I just did it. As it was, they were grateful because they didn't have family in the area and no one to talk to. I ended up helping them through the daunting task of funeral arrangements and sitting with them through the quiet numbing moments until the service took place. As I was leaving their home one day, the mother said to me, "You should check out your insurance policy, you might have a no-fault clause that can help ease some of your financial burdens until you get things squared with the other party's insurance." I turned and looked at her in shock. I hadn't brought the subject up; she had enough problems of her own for me to do that. I could only gather that she had been inspired to pass the message on to me. I guess in my grief, there had been too many other things to worry about and I didn't even consider calling our agent. When I got home, I called him and he chastised me for not calling sooner because we did have a no-fault clause and it covered most of our bills.

Years later, when I began working in the funeral industry, one of my first experiences was going out to the scene of an accident that had claimed the life of a young lady. She had just started driving and decided to take her two friends for a joyride in her father's small pickup. They were obviously having a good time laughing, listening to loud music, and taking the curves of the country roads a little too fast, which propelled them into a ditch and flipped the truck several times, killing her and injuring her friends. The firemen cut her out of the truck, covered her with a tarp, and placed her on the road and waited for us. Her friends had been transported to the hospital before we arrived and she was alone on the road with horrendous injuries from the crushed metal on the truck cab, the most horrific being she had been almost completely scalped.

This case was a very memorable one for me because it was paramount in how I decided to regard my participation in the business. When I lifted the tarp, I saw a young lady that resembled my daughter. She had the color of her hair, her olive skin, and her red toenails. How ironic that this was the case. I had relied on strangers years ago to tend to the needs of my child and often wondered if they had done it with tenderness and compassion, or had they considered it an ordinary day in the death business? I hadn't been able let go of those thoughts until I found myself standing on the highway, preparing to take someone else's precious child, one that reminded me of my own, into my care. I recognized immediately that her injuries would make it a challenge to make her viewable. Yet I knew we would do everything in our power to make it possible. I also realized I was the mother that couldn't be there for my child, but I was there for that one.

The protocol was to transport to the funeral home, take blood and fluid samples, and provide them to the medical examiner so they could determine what the actual cause of death was. I made the choice that as long as I was involved; every family could be assured their loved one was being handled with as much tender loving care as was possible. We arrived at the funeral home, and while trying to remove her blood-soaked clothing and covering her body, we received an urgent call telling us the family was on their way and wanted to see her immediately. We stopped for a minute, looked at each other in panic, and asked if it was possible to make her viewable that quickly. Before I started in the funeral business, I would never have thought myself capable of handling a sight like the one before us, let alone assist in the process of stitching her back together. We quickly gathered what we needed to start the task, and even though we felt rushed, we worked efficiently and quickly, trying our best to spare the family the terrible pain of seeing her in such a wounded condition. I stretched her long blood-drenched hair over her scalp as my partner attempted to sew it back in place. His restorative surgery training was crucial to cases like hers. I was amazed that when reverence and compassion were present, I had the ability to move beyond my uneasiness. I could do it just like I would want someone to do it for one of my loved ones if the tables were turned. It is amazing what we can do when it is our desire to serve.

By the time the family arrived, we had moved her into a viewing room where she looked like an angel sleeping peacefully. What was my gift? My gift was to recognize my value in such a delicate business. I also came to realize that when it came to my grief, I didn't need to continue beating myself up for all the things I should have or could have done if I just had the chance. I had to stop blaming myself for failing to protect my child, and I had to stop paying for mistakes I didn't make. I also felt my child's tender approval when I helped someone else's child. What we can't always do for ourselves, we can sometimes do for others—therein, rests the miracle of service. We can receive comfort knowing that we did what we could when we wanted the same for ourselves. There is an old

Tibetan proverb that says: "When he took time to help the man up the mountain, lo, he scaled it himself."

Acts of service don't have to be the kind that make it on the evening news. Just as we should stop and pay attention to all the miracles that come into our lives on a daily basis, we should pay attention to all the small kind acts of service we can render on behalf of others. Small acts of kindness can make a big difference in someone's life. The opportunities are limitless.

There is great therapeutic value in climbing outside of ourselves especially if we are experiencing troubles of our own. As we do things to help in lightening the burdens of others, comforting the mourners, or listening to those who are troubled or lost, we actually lighten our burdens, comfort our grief, and find our compass for direction. It is the law of the harvest that states: "whatsoever a man soweth, that shall he also reap." If we sow comfort, we will reap comfort. If we sow goodness, we will reap goodness. Mother Teresa said: "The fruit of love is service and the fruit of service is peace."

This chapter could have so easily been merged with the chapter on love because service is about love. If we are to love our neighbor as our self, it would appear that we demonstrate our love for God by loving our fellow man. In the New Testament, Paul admonished us to bear one another's burdens.

Reaching out to others can help us endure our own adversities or find relief in our darkest hours. I felt found when I began to learn this, even though I had been taught this throughout my life, it rang true when I forgot my pain during those moments when I was found in service. We shouldn't have to wait until we have crosses too heavy to bear, but most of us do, and maybe that is why you hear numerous stories of how trials refine people. Don't feel bad if service to others hasn't been on the top of your list or if it seems easier to sit back and weep for what seems to be injustices. There will be times when it will require you to step out of your comfort zone, but you can, and through the act of service you can change the course of your life and your pain. Don't wait for a formal invitation—do it in spite of your anxiety. There are countless opportunities where the sick need buoying up, the poor need help, or the discouraged need a shoulder to lean on. If you choose to help others, it will change you. Ralph Waldo Emerson put it best when he said, "It is one of the most beautiful compensations of life that no man can sincerely try to help another without helping himself."

After I had spent a good deal of time talking with the lady on the phone who didn't want to pay her son's transport bill, her anger had ceased and she had calmed down enough to start asking questions about what she could do. She told me her alcohol use had increased because it was her only way to cope with her husband's impatience. He thought it was time she stop crying. Alcohol was nothing more than a temporary escape, and it wasn't going to do anything to get her through her grief. It would just slow things down and make her become bitter. "Find some way to serve others," I told her. "You will be surprised how it can help you identify and deal with your own pain."

"I don't know how I can," she said warily, "I don't go out much—I'm housebound, my legs are always hurting."

"Start simple," I replied, suddenly feeling a wall in the making and skepticism creeping in, but I went on by telling her she could call someone on the phone that needs cheering up, go to church and find someone who is sitting alone and invite them to sit with her, write letters to lonely people—just start by planting a small seed. "None of it is simple," I went on, "but what options do you have? You can't sprinkle blessings on someone else without the wind blowing a few back on you. Try it."

A willing heart will open many doors and windows that can help you discover where service is needed. Many small acts of kindness can change the world. Many small acts of service can heal our society. The happiest people seem to be those who freely give of their love, their time, and their talents.

It's important to keep in mind that when you think of service and the way it can change your life, it can also change the lives of others. So allow yourself to also be a recipient of service. Learn how to be on the receiving end because by doing so, you are allowing someone else to grow from service, and by doing that, you are still serving.

Service

Journal:
October 6, 1982

Today, I received a letter from Ellie, a dear friend of many years. Our lives seemed to parallel so closely with each other. Our husbands were in the navy together; our first children were born at the same time, and our second within days of each other. We were blessed with many wonderful memories as we traveled the road of being new moms together. Receiving her letter was a comfort, and I could feel her love and support for our family. To have friends willing to reach out and try to help if only they knew how is a spiritual unfolding of faith. It is humbling to reach out and grab hold of an outstretched hand. I also received pictures of Lanette that my sister-in-law photographed. She captured my child for the last time on film, and I am eternally grateful for that. When I receive tender tributes of caring like theirs, I will include them in this journal because I know there will be days when I will find the need to go back and bask in the comfort of their memory.

Dear Kathy and family,

How are you doing? Our prayers and thoughts are constantly with you. I don't know what to say or do to help you through this time. Words are inadequate. What can we do to help?

Lanette will be missed! I was going through our pictures and came across some of the kids together. They are all so precious. If you would like some of them, I'll make sure I have them with me the next time we see you. Our lives have crossed—we became dear friends—and I know we will always share that rare special friendship. Thank you for remembering us in your time of mourning. I feel so bad about not seeing more of you lately. I've missed out on seeing Lanette become a young lady. Time has gone by so fast since you moved.

I know what a joy she was to you and the special place in our hearts that our children have. Children are a real gift, and they are given into our care for such a short time—to be loved and nurtured. Lanette couldn't have been more loved or cared for on this whole earth. Our hearts go out to you all. We love you!

A Legitimate Journey

How is Kristy doing? We pray she'll be able to understand and that time will ease her sorrow over losing her big sister. I've started this letter so many times, both on paper and in my heart. I just want you to know we truly care, and we feel your loss in our hearts. I pray you'll be well and that time will ease your sorrow also. Being human, we grieve for our loved ones — mainly because we have to wait to meet again in heaven.

All our love, Ellie, Steve, Doug, and Danny

We are all connected. When we ask God for his comfort or his help, he takes notice and, many times, sends help through someone else. We should be willing to be his instruments of peace because we all experience service either by being the one to give it or to receive it. Every time we reach out to someone in their time of need, we grow. We never know what the perpetual outcome of any one small act of service can be for someone that crosses our path, but sometimes, it can be immense.

A few years later, Ellie's son, Danny, was tragically murdered in a road rage incident, and then she called me. I was able to share with her things I had learned in my grief. I understood her pain because suddenly her feet were in my shoes. It was crucial for me to let her know that her memories, her love, and her closeness to her son didn't have to fade in order to be able to heal or laugh again. His spirit would always be near her. Ironically, she was the understanding heart in my grief and I was able to be her understanding heart. Do you see the plan? We are here for each other—always.

What will the maze of each one of our lives look like when are given the gift of hovering over to view the whole picture? I am sure it will show that those endless acts of service that were given to help others navigate weren't always easy, but probably necessary for making it out at the other end. Life, whether it is traveled in a maze or on a bumpy narrow road, is meant to be a recurrent reaching out to each other until we finally make a circle. Sometimes, when someone is standing alone in the dark, it is the person who lights the candle that can make the biggest difference. It is within that circle of light that we learn the most. If we stop and pay attention, we will see the miracles that take place within that circle again and again,—miracles that keep teaching us valuable lessons. A treasured example of this was how Randi, Lanette's friend who witnessed her accident, was able to find us after years of searching.

Shortly before this book went to print, and on the anniversary of Lanette's death, my son Bryan spotted a message from her on Facebook and then a beautiful reunion took place. We spoke on the phone and together reminisced about the painful events that affected us both on that fateful day and the days that followed. She wrote me a beautiful letter, one that I will cherish forever, especially since I didn't remember some of the things she says I did, however, it just goes to show how lasting even small acts of caring or service can be.

September 2013

Dear Kathy,

Of all the things you said to me during our first conversation in 30+ years, the statement most poignant for me was that we have come "full circle". For me, this could not be truer. I even started our conversation where we left off by talking about why I stopped coming by your house.

I've thought a lot since then about witnessing Lanette's death, my PTSD and the book you're writing about healing from the most unimaginable and most unbearable grief by helping others. I wondered how Lanette's death impacted my life's work as a therapist specializing in helping those of all ages who have experienced trauma. I had told you about how nobody knew how to help me following her death and how the school had a counselor available to meet with me. She met first with all the other students who had been friends with Lanette—and me last. When I told her that I was fine and didn't want to talk, she dismissed me, relieved to not have to bear witness to my sorrow and pain.

There were many life events that led to my becoming a therapist, but it was only after our conversation that I gained the insight as to how my experience with Lanette's death and how nobody knew how to help me had contributed. Nobody knew how to help me then when I was still a child. Today, I know how to help children who have experienced trauma. They are not alone like I was.

Nobody knew how to help me, but you did. Even in those moments when you were in the depths of your own despair, you reached out to me and provided comfort and nurturing care. It was you who put an arm around my shoulders and walked me to see Lanette as she lay in her casket. It was you who included my friendship with Lanette in the eulogy. I can still hear the male voice speaking about Lanette "coming out of her shell" due to our friendship. It was you who offered me some cherished mementos. It was you who gave me a last picture of her, taken shortly before her death. It was you who wrote on it: Thank you for the beauty of your friendship. And, it was you who welcomed our re-connecting. Which, for me, has been healing and as if I've reconnected with Lanette in some surreal way. And it was you who, once again, facilitated that by providing me comfort and nurturing care.

I am so grateful to have re-connected with you, Kathy.
More than I can adequately express.
With Love, Randi

PS: Words of wisdom I learned from Lanette:
~Always look your best. If you're going somewhere, then someone you want to look good for could also be there.
~When it rains, always look for the rainbow.

How can one rise above the pain
Of the incoming tide,
Or alter the course of a river consumed with pride?
The weak cannot claim victory
Over their troubled wrong
For the victor of forgiveness
Is attributed to the strong.
Be brave and know forgiveness is a virtue
And perhaps you will see the prisoner
You freed was really you.

Forgiveness
A Miracle Tool

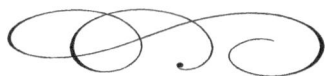

L ost relationships and painful events generated questions of how some people could be so unkind to those they profess to love. It wasn't so much the question as it was the pain that made it play through my mind a million times a day in the beginning. Of course, love is not unkind and love is not abusive and cruel, but those understandings had to arrive in due time and usually on the wings of forgiveness. Forgiveness is not about the other person, the one you are forgiving, as much as it is about you— about freeing up energy and putting it where it can better serve you. For many, it doesn't come easy. Forgiveness is a process, not an instantaneous decision to just let go. For some, forgiveness doesn't require as much processing, but for most, it requires a great deal of faith and courage. There isn't one formula or a "one size fits all" path to forgiveness and letting go.

Set aside the spiritual reasons for a moment and discuss why forgiveness is crucial to physical health. When you hold on to a grudge, a resentment, hostility, anger, or all the other myriad of negative feelings that are toxic, they release hormones like adrenaline and cortisol that have a horrific effect on the cardiovascular and immune system. High levels of adrenaline trigger your platelets to get frazzled, which can lead to heart attacks, stroke, or other cardiovascular illnesses. Who knew? Yet when you forgive, those things settle down and your body returns to self-regulation and self-healing. Just on that knowledge alone, we could end this chapter, but it is not quite so easy to understand, unless you go through the process. The process is what will bring you to a state of healthy forgiveness. Healthy forgiveness is true forgiveness; it comes from the deepest part of the heart. You know forgiveness has been fulfilled when you possess the power to wish the forgiven well.

Nearly everyone has been hurt by someone at one time or another. Some hurts can be small everyday occurrences or large cutting wounds; however, large or small, they can leave you with feelings of anger, bitterness, or even a desire for vengeance. It isn't usually the one that has caused the pain that suffers as much as the recipient who cannot find forgiveness in his heart. It seems like a paradox, doesn't it?

In actual studies, it has been shown that people who are forgiving tend to have better relationships, less stress, fewer health problems, and lower occurrences of serious illnesses. Being unforgiving is caustic, and it raises your blood pressure. Now with barely touching on the physical reasons why we should learn about forgiveness and embrace it, let's talk about the spiritual reasons.

If you are unforgiving, the spiritual price can be even greater. If your life is so wrapped up in the wrong that someone has done against you, bitterness can set in as well as depression and anxiety. Your life begins to look like it lacks meaning or purpose, and you begin to be at odds with your spiritual beliefs or your connectedness with others. Left alone too long to dwell on the hurtful events or situations, vengeance and hostility begin to take root in everything else that you do. That's when negative feelings crowd out positive ones, and before you know it, you are swallowed up piece by piece with your own resentment. I have witnessed people like this and it is scary. It is a testament to the fact that left to its own devices, not forgiving has the ability to destroy life. Not coming to terms with forgiveness can easily cause someone to suffer the same pain over and over again for one hurt or one grievance. Healing is being in the present and holding on to grudges keeps one in the past.

When the pain is so great, how do we get unshackled? From the beginning of time, that has been one of the most difficult questions to answer because it requires a commitment and sincere desire to change and change of heart can be challenging, especially if the person who's hurt you doesn't care if you forgive them. Getting another person to care or change their behavior isn't the point of forgiveness. Think again of it as being more about how it can change your life. Think of how it can bring you the peace and spiritual healing you need to be able to reclaim the power the other person managed to snatch from you.

Here's the good news. You don't have to be Gandhi to start the process. The true essence of forgiveness starts by first accepting that something has already happened and you can't change it. Next, acknowledge that you have been hurt and you still feel upset about it, and then try to look beyond your experience and make the choice to release the weight of the burden for your own benefit. The question then needs to be: what can I do to suffer less? You have choices. You always have choices.

Now, here comes the real paradox. In no way does it mean that we condone, excuse, forget, or deny the offense. It does not mean you have to reconcile with the perpetrator or put yourself back into a relationship or an unsafe environment. It doesn't mean you have to rekindle a friendship or give up the right to seek justice or compensation if someone has caused you great financial loss or severe emotional trauma. Forgiveness simply means you will hand over the justice to God and free yourself of the burden.

A profound lesson in forgiveness hit home with me after being continually hurt by someone I sincerely cared about. I believed I could inspire a change and stop the insanity, so I allowed myself to be victimized until everything abruptly ended. I cried for three months before the hurt gradually shifted to anger. It bogged me down because I didn't have the energy to reclaim my life. I realized I was grieving again and my previous grief work was going by the wayside—plopping me back at square one. I had to take an ugly look in the mirror and admit that anger was not teaching me or building me into a better person. I didn't have the venom that hatred can produce, but I had the fear that unless I found a way out, in spite of the fact that this person had no remorse, no apologies, or no desire to make restitution, it might turn to venom and affect my family and all those that did care for me. I prayed for the strength to just let it go.

One day, I received a phone call from this person. He was in a jam. He was on the verge of losing his vehicle, which he desperately needed to get back and forth to the doctor. It was evident that his health had deteriorated since I had last seen him. My initial gut reaction was: are you kidding—only a fool would care! I didn't owe him a thing. Yet as I was swiftly being carried away with bitterness, a feeling swept over me that I knew was a result of my prayers. The thought that this would be a perfect time to forgive him engulfed me.

"How much are we talking about?" I asked. It was obvious he wanted money.

"Whatever you can spare," he answered, going on to list all the things that were making his life unhappy. I stopped him from sharing his story, it was not necessary for me to know those things. I told him to meet me at the corner in thirty minutes and I would see what I could do. I hung up the phone and sat still for a few minutes before I wrote him check for five hundred dollars, wincing as I did, but I knew it was going to be my ticket to freedom. It wasn't about the money for me as much as it was the token of how hard it was to forgive—I had to give up something to prove it to myself. It had to be sincere.

When I got out of my car and walked toward his, I handed him the check. I wished him well and told him the money was my way of saying I forgive him and I held no grudges. I gave him a quick hug, a hard thing for me to do, but necessary, and I left without looking back. As I drove home, I felt liberated, I felt free, and I was ready to move on—which I did.

A couple of years passed and he came looking for me at a place where he knew I would be. He wanted to tell me something very important. I was hesitant to talk with him, but finally agreed to give him a moment. He seemed calm as I sat down and waited for him to speak. He began by asking me if I could forgive him. He went on to say he was sorry for all the pain he had caused me. He said he believed karma was doing him in. However, none of that mattered to me; my forgiveness had been enough to free me of any emotional connections to him. All I could say to him was I had already forgiven him. I didn't say anything else; I wished him well and left. If I would have waited for him to ask for forgiveness, it might have cost me more than my emotional health. I might have lost my direction and been willing to step right back into the same unhealthy situation. My forgiving him freed me, not his asking me to forgive him. Sometimes, we can justify reasons to postpone forgiveness. One of these is waiting for the perpetrators to repent first, yet such a delay can cause us to forfeit health, happiness, and the wisdom to choose what is best for us. In this particular case, I had to experience what life would be like without letting go of the anger. It wasn't serving me well. It wasn't serving my family well either. Physically, I was falling apart too. I had to pray to be receptive to forgiving, so when the opportunity came to forgive, I could welcome it.

With the forgiveness, I was able to answer my own questions. People that truly love you don't choose to consistently hurt you. That is not love. We must let them go. People make mistakes and are sorry, and we shouldn't hesitate to forgive them, but those who continually cause harm in your life, you can wish them love and send them on their way.

Forgiveness comes more readily when we have faith in God who gives us the strength to withstand some of our greatest challenges, and that is people choosing to hurt us. It also enables us to look beyond ourselves to forgive them. We all suffer injuries from experiences that seem to have no rhyme or reason, and we may never know why some things happen in this life. The reason for it is sometimes only known to God. God knows what we do not know and sees what we do not see. If we can ascend to a higher level of forgiveness in our hearts, we will ascend to a higher level of self-esteem and well-being.

Some of the steps to forgiveness can be:
Understand that forgiveness is for you, not anyone else.

Open up to someone close to you because talking helps you explore your feelings.

Focus on the good things in your life. Learn how to do relaxing mind-body techniques when you find yourself lost in a painful memory.

Concentrate on your personal goals.

Learn how to forgive all those small things people in everyday life do to push your buttons. Don't condone hurtful behavior, but try to understand what led to it.

Try not to take everything too personal. Many times, people don't deliberately target you to cause pain.

Forgive those you love.

Practice first, you might not be ready to say it today, but be ready when it is available to you.

If you never face the person again, forgive them in your heart.

Remember, forgiveness can free you to move forward with your life.

What forgiveness is :
It is about making yourself responsible for how you feel. It is about healing, not about who hurt you.

It is about becoming a hero in your story.

It is about learning how to do it and get good at it. It is a choice.

What forgiveness is not:
It isn't about forgetting what happened.

It isn't about excusing or condoning poor behavior. It is not about denying your hurt.

It is not about reconciling with the offender or waiving the right to justice.

It is not easy.

Forgiveness

What about us desiring forgiveness? Sometimes, that can be more difficult. At one time or another, we will unintentionally hurt someone by either the words we utter or actions that are insensitive. It is part of being human. Yet knowing how to humbly own our mistakes and actions is a vital key to maintaining successful relationships and releasing the pain and shame we may feel. Asking for forgiveness should not be the time to try and figure out how to evenly distribute the blame for something that has happened. Sincere soul-searching should take place prior to asking, because to truly desire forgiveness we should feel remorse. Soul-searching as to why something happened or what the feelings were that triggered the behavior is the groundwork for remorse. If you have ever had to forgive someone to protect your health, then you would know that asking someone to forgive you also helps free them up to let go of the pain you caused them. When you ask for forgiveness and they chose not to forgive, then there is nothing that you can do about it. By sincerely owning your mistake with a resolve to correct it, you are doing the right thing and you deserve to be forgiven. Just remember, some things take time, and depending on the severity of the hurt, forgiveness from another person needs to be in their time.

Forgiving yourself though can be much harder than forgiving someone else or asking someone to forgive you. There are times in life when we believe that we will never be forgiven for falling short of an expectation or unknowingly causing someone else pain that is no longer with us, and therefore, we are tethered to an eternity of self-blame. If you desire someone to forgive you that's deceased or no longer in your life, put it in God's hands; trust me, he will take care of it.

Some people are afraid to forgive themselves because they fear losing their sense of identity and ownership of a transgression. Sometimes, those people who have not developed a strong sense of value in their own lives feel that they constantly need to be reminded how they fall short in the perfection department. Sometimes, we seem to hold ourselves to a higher standard than anyone else around us. Perfectionism can cause us to be too hard on ourselves. Things we would normally forgive others for doesn't apply to us. We can spend a lifetime on many small day-to-day reasons why we just don't measure up and drive ourselves crazy. Removing ourselves from this vicious cycle of thinking is crucial to avoid constantly experiencing the negative emotions that fuel our lack of self-worth and self-forgiveness. When we believe we must be perfect, it will always be a belief that won't deliver.

Letting go of other's expectations for us is conducive to self- forgiveness. We have no control over what others do, say, or think of us, and even though it is difficult not to internalize and believe what really is only someone else's shortcomings, we still need to look into our hearts and know we are doing the best we can. You don't need forgiveness for just being yourself. Forgiving yourself is about feeling bad about specific things, not about who you are as a person. It doesn't mean you should ignore everything and stop trying to improve where you feel improvement is necessary. It just means that you, like all of God's children, are precious enough to know peace. When we forgive ourselves for failing to live according to others' expectations and start following our purpose instead, we will be able to move forward with our own dreams by growing our own set of wings.

Shortly after my daughter's death, I started to attend a support group for families who had lost children, The Compassionate Friends. I remember a lady who shared her story about her inability to forgive herself after her four-year-old daughter drowned in their backyard pool. She told of how the guilt for answering the phone when she did and taking her eyes off her for just three minutes changed her life and changed how she viewed herself as a person who would never be able to be forgiven. She spoke of how she developed such self-loathing to the point where believed she could never be trusted to be a mother again, and being a mother was one of her greatest joys in life. Her feelings were normal. When things like that happen, whether our child dies in a pool, a car accident, or illnesses we weren't able to cure, we tend to think it's because we failed at something. I suffered similar thoughts that tried to convince me that I wasn't a good enough mother, or maybe I should have said yes when I said no, or if only I would have come home earlier or "if only this" or "if only that." Being unable to forgive ourselves for being human is like trying to put out a fire with gasoline. We are human…we make mistakes…we suffer from our mistakes, and then we have to learn how to forgive ourselves so we can do better the next time—and we will do better!

Because we are human, we can get lost in the wilderness of trying to assign blame where it is not justified. If we can't find a reason to blame ourselves, then we usually come up with a reason to be angry at someone else—maybe because they aren't grieving as intensely as we are or we believe they just didn't love as deeply as we did. To understand that all people grieve differently is a step in the right direction of getting over the blame hurdle. Placing blame or guilt on anyone, including ourselves, only deepens our wounds. Realize also that men and women usually grieve differently. Just because men are known to speak fewer words doesn't mean their hearts are any less broken.

Healing came to the woman whose daughter drowned in her pool when someone pointed out to her that unless she purposely held her child underwater, she deserved forgiveness. If her child came back to give her a message, she would say the same thing. To heal, it is crucial to find forgiveness for ourselves and for those around us. It takes courage to admit mistakes or misconceptions and it takes even more to ask for forgiveness or to give it whether someone wants it or not. Remember when I said that this journey required courage? Unwillingness to forgive keeps you on that scary little dirt road. You can't turn around and you can't change the past, but with the miracle of forgiveness, you can change the future.

Laughter, It can come quickly or unexpected,
Magnificent, glorified making our soul rise,
Lifting our hearts above our sorrow
So love cannot hide behind a dark disguise.
We should seek it, not deny it,
For it is like the sun that makes winter warm,
Like the courage it takes to seize a chance.
Gentle humor Is God's medicine,
For He desires we laugh and while we're at it, dance!

Laughter
A Tool to Lighten Your Burden

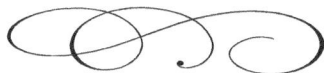

H ow can you think of laughter when you are in so much pain? Catch yourself laughing and guilt springs up like a weed in a moist spring garden. I can't remember how long I went before I allowed myself to laugh again—that is without feeling guilty. The phrase, "I'll never laugh again," is perhaps one that you hear people say the most when they are thrown into grief. If you tell someone that laughter is the best medicine when they have just been knocked off their feet, they will no doubt look at you like you're crazy. Who feels like laughing when their world has just fallen apart? Giving ourselves permission to laugh during times of grief is very difficult to do. But laughter can support the healing process and raise us up. Here is what I have learned about laughter: It is absolutely a gift from God!

There are times in life when our fire goes out and needs to be rekindled. Who can say exactly how that has to happen, but there are miracles that take place every day that help lift and rekindle hope, and laughter is one of them. Never feel guilty for feeling joy or letting laughter lift your spirit.

Abraham Lincoln once said, "With the fearful strain that is on me night and day, if I did not laugh I should die."

Even in the most difficult of times, laughter can lift us. It is a powerful antidote to pain, illness, and stress—and grief is stressful, yet nothing works faster to bring your emotions into balance than a good laugh. Humor does lighten your burdens, it inspires hope and keeps you connected to other people and in times of sadness, that is very important.

Laughter relaxes the body by relieving physical tension and stress and it also helps boost your immune system by increasing immune cells and infection-fighting antibodies. Grief is hard on the immune system and needs to be addressed with all of the knowledge and tools that are available to us. Laughter triggers the release of endorphins, which are the body's natural feel-good chemicals. It also protects the heart by increasing blood flow, helping to protect you from cardiovascular problems.

More than just a break from sadness and pain, laughter can actually boost your courage, giving you the strength to find sources of hope. Even in the most difficult times, a laugh, or simply a smile can do wonders toward making you feel better. Laughter helps to reclaim healthy emotional balance. Sometimes, laughter can lift a burden even if it is only for a moment.

If you haven't thought of this before, do it now: laughter is your birthright! It is a natural part of life that is innate in us all. Even infants begin interacting first with a smile and then, within months, full laughter. If a baby is in the house, you will more than likely hear laughter.

Happiness is what we pursue in life. Joy is a state of the spirit and the conviction of the mind. What a man is may largely be determined by his greatest quest. People's happiness or misery depends upon what they seek and the choices they make. There are seeds of happiness, laughter, and joy planted in every one of us and our mental attitude and disposition decides what environment we give them so they may germinate. There is as much need for sunshine in the spirit as there is for sunshine in the world. People need encouragement and cheer. It is not only for the already happy ones or those that have never known tragedy or human suffering. It is for everyone and the warm glow of the heart at peace with itself is the design within that God wants us to aspire to. Laughter, simply put, is spiritual sunshine.

If laughter has not come easy to you or you feel guilty for indulging in it, how can you weave it back into your life to partake of its healing power? Begin by seeking it out and build from there. Read things that inspire humor like perhaps "Laughter the Best Medicine" in Reader's Digest or watch a funny movie, pick up the comics, or when you hear a group of people laughing, move closer—most people are happy to share their humor because it gives them an opportunity to laugh again. Observe children playing, listen to their laughter, and observe their light hearts. Learn to laugh at yourself and surround yourself with others who love to laugh. Get a pet—especially a kitty, and enjoy their innocent playfulness. Albert Schweitzer said: "The only escape from the miseries of life is music and cats," but I say, add smiles to that because smiling is the beginning of laughter. Some adults become accustomed to containing instinctual reactions to laugh, but by resisting the urge, they also reduce the joy. It is okay to laugh, even in public. Another way to get closer to laughter is to count your blessings because feeling gratitude distances you from negative thoughts, and if you are not feeling sad, you have less distance to travel with your emotions to arrive at joy.

Each of us during our lives will be touched by grief. It might be through the death of a loved one, divorce, illness, or perhaps sharing the grief of a friend or loved one. If you lost a loved one, think of them, pull out your good memories—think of the times when they said something funny or did something funny, and then smile with the memory. We all have moments in our lives when someone has touched us with their smiles and their humor. Should we forget those times or should we cherish them? How could we have shared love with them in all its fullness if we never laughed with them?

Be assured that in grief, there is a place for every emotion— even laughter. Laughter is an effective way to help with brain function and memory retention. So smile at your memories and be grateful for them because there is not a lost loved one who would want us to remain miserable and unhappy and to never again know laughter. There is an old proverb that says: "If you are too busy to laugh, you are too busy."

I believe God has a sense of humor and I believe the angels laugh. What does humor and divine presence have in common? We can't see them with the naked eye, but we can experience them within our hearts. Humor is like the light, when it is present, fear and darkness must take a backseat. Anne Frank wrote: "Think of all the beauty still left around you and be happy."

If laughter does so many positive things for the body and the soul, would not our Creator also partake of it? Laughter is like God putting his hands on our shoulders and helping to steady us.

"The truth is laughter always sounds more perfect than weeping. Laughter flows in a violent riff and is effortlessly melodic. Weeping is often fought, choked, half strangled, or surrendered to with humiliation."
—Anne Rice

True laughter has an essence of love, and God is all about love. Red Skelton said: "No matter what your heartache may be, laughing helps you forget it for a few seconds"

"If you wish to glimpse inside a human soul and get to know the man, don't bother analyzing his ways of being silent, of talking, of weeping, or seeing how much he is moved by noble ideas; you'll get better results if you just watch him laugh. If he laughs well, he's a good man...All I claim to know is that laughter is the most reliable gauge of human nature." 8
—Fyodor Dostoyevsky

People can sit in silence and we don't know what they are thinking. We know a frown can suck the energy out of a room. We can look at the tears of someone and feel compassion for their situation, but when we witness laughter, our hearts feel lighter. It is like music to the soul. That is why so many great speakers will begin with humor to put their audiences at ease and help them be emotionally receptive to their message.

So let down your guard, wave the guilt away, and if a smile or a moment of sure bliss and laughter flows your way, it's a medicine, it's a tool, use it, enjoy it, because you are human you were designed for it.

If you pay attention to the strength
Of the body you live in,
It is only as strong as the spirit that resides within.
Health and wisdom, the reward of being whole,
Is achieved with balance between
The body and the soul.

Health
A Tool of Wisdom

ithin the beginning years of my grief, my physical health slowly but steadily declined. I was young—only in my thirties, and relatively healthy. I didn't drink, I didn't smoke, I didn't even abuse Aspirin or Tylenol, and I was dedicated to feeding my family healthy meals.

Over the course of the following four years, my grief continued to deepen with the loss of my mother, the loss my baby boy, Jeremy, and relationship problems. Was it any wonder my body began to fall apart? It began with fatigue, then gastrointestinal nuisances, and then escalated to miscarriages, nightmares, weight loss, weight gain, coughs, and colds and every virus that came along, all of which made life even more difficult. As time progressed, I developed sores and blisters that covered the back of my throat and the roof of my mouth and my doctor didn't have a clue what caused them, yet by the time I aggressively visited him demanding answers, every joint in my body ached beyond what any over the counter pill could touch. Then a mammogram revealed a lump in my left breast and I was referred to a specialist who told me that if I were his wife, he would suggest I go in for a biopsy and be prepared for a mastectomy. Breast cancer! I remember screaming inside with fury, that's what took my mother! My doctor also disclosed that my blood tests didn't look good either. "If something doesn't change with whatever is going on in your life," he stated with certainty, "you are a good candidate for dying young. One more thing," he added as he grabbed his clipboard and walked out of the room, "I think you need to see a psychiatrist."

I heard that grief was hard on the body, but I didn't realize how hard until I despairingly observed my own falling apart piece by piece. I was being handed a bum rap in life, and there wasn't anything I could do about it—so I thought.

If grief is a natural reaction to loss, can it kill us? A lot of people in the anguish of their grief express an indifference to wanting to live anyway so as health declines they might not care one way or the other. I suffered with those feelings on more than one occasion; however, reality kicked in when I was cautioned that maybe I wouldn't live, so I had to seriously stop, look beyond myself toward my children, and realize I needed to live and I needed to take action before it was too late.

Even though grief is a natural response to loss, we have to learn to get through it. If we think we can close our eyes or ignore it—the truth is, it can kill us. Grief should be given the same attention that any ailment, whether physical or emotional, is given. When we feel helpless or hope-less, the worst thing to do is look the other way or just stand back and hope someone will rescue us. One of the important principles to keep in mind about holistic health is that we cannot nor should we try to separate our physical health from our emotional, mental, or spiritual health. They are all connected, and when one is not well, our disharmony brings us into a state of disease. So when we have a physical disorder, we need to look deeply into our emotional feelings and our thoughts and attitudes in order to find ways to restore our natural harmony and bring balance into our life.

As I drove home from the doctor's office, I felt defeated. It was at that time I realized that in spite of all my pain and in spite of all the times I had asked God to just stop my heart; I didn't really want to die. I felt selfish when I thought of my precious children that still needed their mother. I humbly realized the need to surrender my life into the hands of someone wiser than I was. It was the only hope I had of rescuing myself, and on the Superstition Freeway that afternoon, I cried a prayer.

When I arrived home, it was approaching the dinner hour, yet before I could think about cooking, I had an intuition that I needed to be alone for a while—I needed a place where quietness and solitude could embrace me. I glanced at the closet under the stairs and went in. I pulled the chain on the dim light and sat on the floor and wept.

As I sat in the dimly lit harbor of my sanctuary, I noticed the large chest that was beckoning my attention. I opened it and began reminiscing over the memories it held inside. I thought about my mother and her last days and our discussions on health and the book we talked about. The book!—I sat up straight— where was it? Then I remembered I had loaned it to Karen, a young twenty-three-year-old acquaintance from my church because she was battling lung cancer. I couldn't remember how long ago it had been, but then, I wondered if she had even read it. I started to wipe away my tears as I felt a warm feeling of peace enter my heart, and I knew what I had to do. I needed to get the book, read it again, and start the process of learning how to earnestly approach my healing. As I thought about the challenge before me, the ring of the phone ruthlessly interrupted my thoughts. I waited to see if someone else would answer it, and when no one did, I stepped out of the closet and grabbed it. "Hello, Kathy," a male voice resonated over the line, "this is Karen's husband, you may not know me, but Karen asked me to call you."

I wiped a few more tears off my face with the back of my hand, hardly believing what I was hearing and slowly lowered myself to the floor. "How is Karen?" I asked. "Did she ever read the book I gave her?"

"Yes, she did," he answered, "that is why I am calling. She doesn't want to go through chemotherapy, she wants to go to the Gerson Hospital in Mexico, but if I am to pay for it, I will need to stay here and work." There was a pause and his breathing got heavy. I waited through the silence—anxiously waiting for him to interrupt it. He took a deep breath, "She wants to know if you can go with her. The hospital requires everyone to bring a companion that can stay with them, learn how the therapy works, and be able to help them when they return home." He continued on as if he were trying to sell me a used car. "I will take care of everything, pay for your stay and your plane fare if you agree to go. She is failing fast and time is critical." I could sense he wasn't happy about her choice, but he let me know he wasn't going to stand in her way, because after all, it was her life.

"Of course I will help!" I hastily answered before my brain had a chance to process what he was actually asking me to do or the coincidence that I had just been weeping on the closet floor and wondering about her. Compared to hers, my ailments didn't seem like much more than a scraped knee. For a miraculous moment, not by my conscious choice though, the weight of my afflictions seemed trifle. Noting his sense of urgency, I agreed to make arrangements for the care of my children so I would be ready to fly out with her in the morning. He graciously expressed his gratitude and hung up. I stood there staring at the phone in my hand and wondering if I had just become an instrument in one of God's miracles. I dried my eyes and remember thinking: Okay, okay, I've got time, I'll help Karen get on her feet to healing, and when she is on her way, I will take the time to start on mine.

The proper care of the body is indispensable in healthy living. For life to be at its best, the body needs to function properly. So why does grief affect our health? Studies show that grief does compromise the immune system, leaving the door open for illness to creep in and take hold. It lowers the white cell count,thereby increasing these risks probably more so than at any other time,in our lives. Colds, viruses, joint pain, high blood pressure, and heart problems rear their ugly heads more often in grief than at other times. Prolonged immune disorders increase risks tenfold and affect the overall health and physical well-being of people all the time, and when the physical health suffers, the spiritual health suffers as well. It's all connected.

Depression is usually a part of the grief process and can cause sadness, insomnia, lack of appetite, weight loss, or weight gain. It is considered normal with grief, yet if the person does not heal within a reasonable amount of time, and who can say what reasonable is, it can become permanent. It is at that time when professional intervention should be taken whether it is in the form of therapy, medical help, or committing to a healthier lifestyle or better nutrition. Because grief can invade every element of your life, it needs to end at some point.

There is actually a syndrome that is called the broken heart syndrome that is called Takotsubo Cardiomyopathy. It is a type of heart failure that is caused by grief or severe stress. It can cause the left ventricle to balloon out and take an unusual shape. The symptoms can mimic a heart attack except electrocardiograms do not always show the problem. One experiences chest pain, shortness of breath, and arm pain in much the same way as a heart attack, but it is different. Many times, post-menopausal women who are grieving are more likely candidates for this if they have lost a long-time mate or relationship and their grief doesn't subside within a certain amount of time. The good news is that it usually takes less time for recovery than it does a heart attack. But it is not a myth when you hear someone comment, "She or he died of a broken heart."

Grief does affect your energy level, so finding the strength you need to overcome exhaustion can be difficult. The work of grief requires a lot of energy and fatigue is very common, but as you work through the process, it will improve with time. Just try to recognize when your body tries to tell you it is in need of extra special attention. Respond by taking your first step whether you feel like it or not by getting the nutrition and exercise you need and professional help if necessary. There has been a lot of headway made in the past twenty or thirty years that has enlightened the medical and mental community to understand with greater awareness the impact grief has on people and how to help them weave their life back together.

I got my book back from Karen, and throughout the years, it has been passed around several times. Its cover is worn, its pages bent, and some lives changed by it. It was written by a lady back in the seventies named Jaquie Davison called *Cancer Winner*. It biographed her journey from illness to diagnosis and then her discovery of the doctor Max Gerson who, years before, began research about healing people with nutrition—people who had been sent home to die with no hope of recovery. He learned the value of fresh fruit and vegetable juices and diets that helped detox and clean the liver so it could do the work that God had intended it to do. He believed our bodies were magnificent creations that were capable of healing almost every illness if brought back into balance and he dedicated his life to proving it with a great deal of success.

My sister, Diana, was waiting at the San Diego Airport to give us a ride over to the Gerson Institute in Bonita where Norman Fritz, the co-founder and executive vice president of the Gerson Hospital and the

Gerson Institute, waited to give us a ride to the hospital in Mexico. At that time, the United States did not allow unorthodox methods like nutrition to treat cancer; therefore, their hospital was not approved nor allowed in the States.

I stayed the recommended three weeks with Karen, sat in on the lectures, learned about food preparation, and met several people who were actually beating the disease. I got close to Karen and grew to love her fighting spirit and felt blessed that she had given me the opportunity to participate and learn firsthand how the therapy worked. I often wondered when I used to talk with my mother if I would ever have the fortitude to pick up the book and study it enough to understand and implement the knowledge. While in Mexico, I took advantage of every learning moment I had been blessed to be a part of and it empowered me and gave me hope.

I witnessed the love everyone at the hospital and those back at the institute had for their patients, and a day didn't go by that inspiring moments passed by me without grabbing at my heart strings and yanking on them. I was kept in awe.

Journal:

September 24, 1986

Diana hitched a ride with Norm to spend the day with us and sit in on some of his lectures. She was excited to see Karen and see how she was doing. I had explained to her that her pain throughout the night had worsened. Her right side was giving her the most grief, and she couldn't find a comfortable to position in which to lie. I was hoping it was because she was having a healing reaction, but I wasn't sure. I told Diana we were both getting homesick and I missed my kids, but the knowledge I was receiving was worth it all just to be there.

After the lecture, Norm asked me how Karen was doing and I said she was in a lot of pain. He said he was going to go up to her room and see if he could do something to ease it. He went on ahead and I followed a few minutes later.

I stepped into the room and it was completely engulfed in silence. I felt like an intruder, but quietly went in and sat on my bed. I watched as Norm placed his hands on different parts of her body, and when they came to a rest, he applied pressure. He quietly did this for about ten minutes while Karen sat upright in her bed with her head cradled in her hands. There was a new energy in the air, one that was unfamiliar, but I knew it was positive. When Norm finished, he stepped over by the end of the bed and was flexing his hands as if he had just given them a rough workout.

Karen raised her head out of her hands, coughed a little, and looked up with this big smile on her face. "It worked!" She laughed with excitement. "I don't know what you did, but it worked, my pain is gone. Thank you! Thank you!"

Norm nodded in recognition of her gratitude, smiled, then paused for a moment and commented that he saw a negative darkness where the head of her bed was. He moved closer, took hold of the end of it, and moved it away from the wall about three feet. He stood silent for a moment just studying her and then told her she radiated an inner light. I had been as quiet as a church mouse up to that point, but I couldn't resist asking if he meant a spiritual light. He said, "Yes." Then he looked over at my bed and told me I should move my bed away from the wall as well because the same negative darkness was across the head of my bed. I jumped up and scooted my bed away from the wall without giving it a second thought. A man who could so gently take Karen's pain away didn't have to say anything to convince me that I'd be better off moving my bed as well. He gave Karen a hug before he left the room, and as soon as he stepped out, we both let out a sigh and spoke of the love we felt while he was in there.

Here is the irony of this whole experience. Upon arriving home, Karen seemed to be doing just great. I went over to her house each day and helped prepare her food, make her juices, and administer her B-12 injections. It was a challenge—at times, I got very tired, but somehow, the strength showed up when I needed it the most and my family managed fine with my absence—which was a blessing. The whole time I was at the hospital, and upon returning, I tried to follow the same eating plan and I began to feel better. Eating better food contributed to my energy—I had to admit that much.

We had been home about a month and it was a crisp Sunday morning when I arrived to start Karen's morning juices and her husband met me at the door. I had become accustomed to knocking, then just letting myself in, but this time, he cracked the door as if purposely trying to block my entrance.

"We won't need your help any longer," he told me, trying to avoid eye contact with me. At first, I didn't know what to say. I felt speechless. Then I choked out the question.

"Why?" I wanted an answer, a good one; because I felt she had been doing so well.

"To make a long story short," his voice cracked, "we had a fight, she went home to her mother's, and we are calling a lawyer." He shut the door.

I stood frozen on the porch for a while with my jaw open like a Venus fly trap and felt panic begin to swell in the pit of my stomach. I hurried home and tried to call her, but she was resting and I was told to call back later. I was a nervous wreck for most of the day until I finally got her on the phone. "Karen," I pleaded, "don't give up. I will still help you, I've got a spare room, and you can stay at my house and just concentrate on getting better."

"I can't do that," she said. "That would be asking way too much."

"No," I pleaded like a grounded child, hoping for a second chance. "I will help you get better, and then you can help me get better. It won't be too much, you are young you deserve it."

"No, Kathy," she firmly admonished, "I am tired and I don't want to fight this any longer."

I was beside myself when I hung up the phone. I called Norm in tears and asked him to call her and talk some sense into her.

Norm didn't call her; instead, he caught a plane and flew over to see her. Together, we went over to her mother's house to pay her a visit. We went in, and after a while, Norm asked for time alone with her. I left the room and went outside, sat under a large tangerine tree on the front lawn, and waited. The tangerines were ripe and falling to the ground. I peeled a couple of them and ate the sweet fruit, and viewed the tree with a new-found appreciation. Right in front of me was the sweet bounty of nutrients that God created to feed our bodies.

When Norm came out, he sat under the tree with me and peeled a tangerine for himself and said he told Karen it was okay to let go because she had fought a courageous fight.

For a minute, I looked at him in disbelief. I wanted him to talk her into fighting. I wanted her to succeed and show the world that nutrition could heal and miracles worked.

A week later, I visited her in the hospital. She was thin, her eyes were dark and hollow—I hardly recognized her. It was the last time I saw her. She passed away a couple of days later. As we talked, both of us knew it was good-bye. I told her I was troubled and didn't understand why it was ending this way. I was sure it was a miracle when she asked for my help. We were going to show the world it worked. She just looked at me and smiled. I realized after she died that the miracle did work, but it was for me. The light Norm spoke of suddenly became very clear to me. I saw its fullness, and love filled my heart because Karen appeared as the answer to a prayer I had cried and because I answered her call, I was blessed. God didn't waste a minute. Karen, I am sure, willingly took on the assignment to be the angel my life was in desperate need of.

I went home, put my family on a nutritional healing diet, and my son, Bryan, and I did the less intensive Gerson therapy for well over a year and became stronger and healthier than I could ever remember. The therapy helped restore Bryan's immune system and what had once been a frail little body of infections,colds, and life-threatening childhood illnesses became a strong active body that for the rest of his childhood didn't require a single dose of antibiotics or hospital stays. I had the energy to start walking, enjoy more music, and to begin writing.

I couldn't wait to go back to my doctor and have them redo all the tests because I knew what I learned and what I practiced made a difference. As my body grew stronger, so did my spirit.

A Legitimate Journey

I still remember the words of my doctor. "I don't know what you did, but you have the blood of someone that will probably live to be a hundred or more."

The pain from my grief didn't disappear, but my body became stronger and I had more hope that getting through it was possible. Getting the nutrients your body needs to fight off illness is a crucial tool in helping to get through grief. Sometimes, women who are the caretakers in the family and the ones that prepare the food find it even more difficult to eat right because they simply don't have the energy to work in the kitchen. If someone asks how they can help, suggest helping with their family's nutrition. If you are the one grieving—please ask for help. Until enough strength returns to handle the daily chores of nutritional management, supporting family members can be a great source of help with food preparation, shopping, and education. During grief, it takes more than calories to keep someone alive, it takes nutrients, ones that God designs especially to heal. Just as it is essential to feed the soul, it is essential to feed the body. Learning what to eat and what not to eat is crucial in a crisis.

Too many people during grief are literally taken into bondage with ill health because they don't take the time to eat right. In our world of fast foods, quick microwaveable meals, and soda pop, getting enough nutrition to ward off diseases and build our immune system can be a daunting task. Yet our needs are great when it comes to healing and finding that proper balance between our physical and spiritual needs. We pop pills for every ailment without asking what nutrient our body is missing. Everything is about ease until our health becomes a state of disease, and we can't imagine why. Our foods are full of toxins and chemicals to preserve them so that they have a long shelf life. We eat out of cans that have no nutrients or enzymes left in them. Sometimes even bugs or animals won't touch them.

Our bodies were created with the ability to heal and restore, yet year after year, if we neglect to give it the proper nutrients, it cannot and won't function well. Hunger and appetite are two different things. Hunger is our physiological need for food, and appetite is usually developed from some kind of unmet emotional need. Add stress, depression, and grief and you have a calamity waiting to happen. If you are eating the kind of foods that cause inflammation, as most refined grains and sweets do, it will manifest in your life as some kind of illness. Heart disease, diabetes, immune disorders, and obesity develop through time by unhealthy habits; they are not instantly caught like the flu or a virus, but they can disable and they can end life.

Take a look at nature; it should inspire you to know what is best for your body. The human body can take a little abuse, and sometimes, it is just pure bliss to eat something sinfully sweet that is full of sugar and fat, but the largest percent of what we should consume should be as close to nature as possible. Only let a small percentage be touched by other humans and sold in a supermarket with a long shelf life. Eat abundantly live whole foods, try to breathe clean air, and drink clean water. Avoid as many toxins as you can because toxins are the culprits that make your liver work harder than it should. Remember, the liver is also responsible for cleaning your blood and balancing your minerals. If you consume too many toxins, your liver can't do the other jobs of cleansing and healing your cells. Try to add as many fresh greens to your diet, fresh vegetables along with beans, nuts, and seeds. They are the heroes of physical health.

So what about my mammogram? A new one a year later showed that the lump was still there, but it hadn't grown or shown any signs of calcification or malignancy. I have had my regularly scheduled physicals and kept an eye on it for over thirty years, but when I got the phone call to help Karen, I knew I was going to be all right. Miracle? I think so!

Nature is God's handiwork on this earth.
A breeze, a tree, or a flower opening
Its petals to greet the morning sun,
All rejoice with love for
The splendid things God has done.

Nature
A Tool of Appreciation

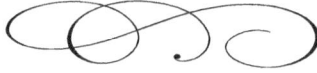

I n the presence of nature, a spirit of pleasure usually runs through man in spite of his sorrows, so embracing nature face to face can aide in healing. Its beauty testifies that divinity is present and witnesses that it was created for us, and we are part of it and part of God. It speaks to our soul. To truly appreciate nature, we must pay attention and to listen to it, for if we do, we will know it is glad to be with us.

Nature, whose creation and beauty move through and around us like an electrically charged flow of energy, invites us to partake of its powers to heal, to feed, and to inspire. It works and moves harmoniously together in absolute rhythm and perfection, for God is forever artistically pouring himself out with every beautiful creation. His ceaseless activity and his divine love promise us the continuity of earth and its beauty. Beauty is what God gives us as we seek to understand him. Whenever snow falls or blue skies are adorned with white fluffy clouds, we should not miss the opportunity to see the beauty. When rain labors to open the new buds of spring or birds fly through the heavens, stop and see his love manifested in plain view.

Our spirits can find joy in the beauty of nature if we stop and pay attention for a genuine moment and observe the most obvious things like the stars, the trees, the flowers, or the grass under our feet, the snow-capped mountains or the valleys with its mantle of pure glistening snow. In the spring, beautiful families of tulips or little purple pansies peeping through the snow to catch the rays of the morning sun or the sweet per-fume of flowers in the summer, songs of birds, or the ripening grain can truly enhance our lives and stir our hearts to reverence. Imagine going beyond just the obvious and look at the earth and every living plant and creature and see how they are all connected.

When you experience the reverence that the spiritual impressions of nature gives you, your mind will open to its influence and awaken you—you may even begin to feel you have arrived home. The truth is, you are home for the earth was designed to be your home and to experience life. The earth and the universe is the property of every individual, and if we desire, it can be our dowry and personal estate. It is right to respect it and desire to take care of it.

Where can you go to find solitude? There are times in our lives when we need to retire from society, to give up cramped workspaces, trapped still air or the perpetual racket that rouses us to seek sanctuary. Where is the best place to go? We can't always run away from our problems, but we can run toward places that give us beauty and calmness and the wisdom to see things clearly. It is in nature, a medicinal marvel, and a displayer of beauty that we can find places to listen with gratitude and observe with reverence so we may understand what we need to know to achieve balance of the body and spirit. For the true lover of nature, it is not a question, but a foregone conclusion that nature is a way to divinely touch the soul. Like God, it is available every hour and every season and shows its delight equally well during the darkness of midnight or the brightness of the noonday sun. Nature is anywhere that God has used his handiwork on the earth by creating beauty, usefulness, and harmony for the delight and well-being of man. For some, it can be experiencing the desert floor and admiring the way the heat and light give life to a cactus and beauty to rock formations and to others it can be locked into the beauty of a forest of trees where barely a stream of light may shine through to reveal a crystal blue sky. Nature can be a breeze that stirs the air enough to brush over a troubled brow or the scent of a rose that brings a memory of a pleasant time. It can be one thing to someone and something else to another, but the effects can be similar to the soul.

God constantly speaks to us through nature. Think of the rainbow and its beauty and listen for the message your heart receives. He shows us the metamorphic transition of the caterpillar into a butterfly and we can relate it to our transformation and progression as we experience earth life. We are assisted by natural objects in God's expression all the time. How great a language it is to hear from the beauty and solace of the earth? Have you ever thought how often we let the mountains, the oceans, or the skies give significance to our thoughts? We employ them all the time as emblems and similes in relationship to our lives and our purpose. We may say, "I feel like I am adrift on a storm-tossed sea or struggling to find my way out of the wilderness." All of nature is a metaphor to the human mind and a teacher of many lessons. If we paid attention, we would see that we have more teachers and servants waiting on us than we ever imagined. The virtuous understand that they are served by nature and the beauty of every lesson and every meaning. Nature is constantly trying to reveal its treasures, open our eyes, and enlighten our minds. Influence constantly breathes from every sight and sound that comes from its existence. The light of higher laws shines through the universe, and if we start to acknowledge and enjoy it, it will become transparent. When it does, we are seeing with the light and there is peace seeing with the light.

I remember talking once with someone who had just visited the Grand Canyon, and he said standing on the edge and looking down made him feel so insignificant, yet I feel that when we understand that we are all a part of the same creation and it was created for our spirits to behold, it teaches us that we are magnificent, not insignificant.

Man is not himself only...He is all that he sees;
all that flows to him from a thousand sources. He is the land,
the lift of the mountain lines, the reach of its valleys.
—Mary Austin

When we find ourselves in the darkness of grief, it is sometimes difficult to look around and challenge ourselves to make a connection with the earth, or because of our grief, we may find ourselves desiring it more than ever. When we ask for ways to help us cope and we seek to understand, we may be inspired to find the solace that nature can provide. To seek the refuge of nature is like surrendering our whole being to witness what it has to say.

A Legitimate Journey

Throughout life, I have learned that one of the best medicines I have to help with dark times or loneliness is to simply go outside. I love to be around trees, and when I look at the blue sky filled with white fluffy clouds, I want to pick up a paint brush and create the same picture. I feel beautiful when I look at flowers and joyous when I see dewdrops on the plants in the morning; it makes me feel I need not thirst after anything. When I see leaves dancing in the wind, I want to dance, and when I hear a bird, I want to sing. When my heart is full with these things, I feel loved. Anne Frank, locked in the small fearful confines of her sequestered prison, wrote how her best remedy for feeling lonely or unhappy was to go outside where she could be alone with the heavens, nature, and God. She said she believes God wishes to see people happy amidst the simple beauty of nature, for only then can we get the feeling that all is as it should be with God. Imagine her being confined where she wasn't able to be out and partake in the solace that nature provides. I'm sure missing it only confirmed the power of it, at least enough for her to write about it.9

When I moved to the Northwest, I was in awe of its beauty. I was warned by a few people upon my leaving the drier climate of Arizona and California that I would come to hate the relentless rain and probably wish I had not moved. In the beginning, I viewed the rain as a metaphor for tears that I hoped could help wash some of the pain from my heart and soap that could give me clean air to breathe. Yet as time went on, I grew to love it for many other reasons like how it cleaned the air to give us the deep blue skies, the green it gave the fields and the abundant blossoms in springtime, all of which made me realize this was the place God wanted me to be. Albert Einstein said to look deep into nature, and if we did, we would understand everything.

I've seized opportunities to visit many beautiful monuments the Northwest is known for, and I have many more to visit, but so far, the one that brought me the deepest connection with my Maker was when I visited Oregon's Crater Lake. I was invited to take the trip up the mountain with my friend, and of course, I jumped at the opportunity since it had been on my list of places I wanted to see, but I was not prepared for the way if affected me. Had I known it had the ability to inspire such gratitude, I would have visited it much sooner. Even though I had seen pictures, I realized that the lake had to be personally experienced.

Crater Lake was formed in a volcanic crater. It is the deepest lake in the United States and is fed solely by falling rain and snow. It has no inflow or outflow at the surface, which makes it also one of the clearest lakes in the world.

When I got out of the vehicle and looked over the crest of the volcano, the clear deep peaceful water reflected the serene blue sky and I was blown away by the glorious euphoria I felt, which quickly turned to a humble feeling of reverence. There were no boats, water skiers, or people swimming in it, but it didn't surprise me because I couldn't imagine anyone wanting to interfere with the divine stillness. My heart began to swell with appreciation for its majestic beauty. It was like seeing a reflection of heaven. Understanding heaven was within my grasp.

If you were able to travel the world and search for all the beautiful gifts of beauty we are given, the numbers would be too great to count, but they spiritually touch someone somewhere and that is how God intended it to be. I would encourage everyone to take the opportunity to find some of those places and be inspired to be connected to your creator. Charles Cook wrote that our deepest roots are in nature. It doesn't matter who we are or where we live, and it doesn't even matter what kind of life we lead because we are all linked with the whole creation.

What a joy it is to feel the soft, springy earth under my feet once more,
to follow grassy roads that lead to ferny brooks where I can bathe my fingers in a
cataract of rippling notes, or to clamber over a stone wall into green fields
that tumble and roll and climb in riotous gladness!
—Helen Keller

Going outside and standing barefoot on the grass or soil can connect us with the unlimited energy that the earth conducts through its charged electrons. It is healing to walk barefoot on a beach and let the waves tickle your toes. Hiking the path of a mountain, holding a kitty, and sitting in the rain can all be therapeutic. You can only know these things by experiencing them. The real gifts of nature come when you take the time to tune into it and listen. It you stay still long enough with an open heart, it will tell you what your spirit wants to know, and it can comfort you.

Wild animals that are wounded will retreat to a secluded spot and lay on the ground so their body is pressed against the earth to help the healing process. The more a child plays outdoors, the calmer their behavior is. Richard Jefferies wrote that if you want to inspire in your children deep thoughts or holy emotions, let them experience the freedom of the meadows or to walk the hills because they can purify us. Even Walt Whitman wrote that the secret of making the best people is to let them grow in the open air and eat and sleep with the earth.

If you want to live in the light and you want to find your joy again, you cannot overlook nature because it would be to overlook life and purpose and understanding. To walk through grief, walk through it with the assurance that all is okay with the world, with God, with you, and with your loved ones. When you see a rainbow, remember the promise that God's hands are in everything and his promises are eternal. When you see new birth in the springtime, know that everything renews, just as your joy can. Mahatma Gandhi put it so eloquently when he said: "The purpose of life is undoubtedly to know oneself. We cannot do it unless we learn to identify ourselves with all that lives. The sum- total of that life is God."

Rainbows (Written for Lanette)
You loved rainbows, until now, I never questioned why.
Was it because of the colors, or the way the sun set on them
When seen through the clouds of a rain-drenched sky?
You loved rainbows that much I knew.
Why? Was there a symbol or something they stood for,
Or just a sense of wonderment to you?
Was I too blind to love rainbows, love them like you always did?
Did you see something I didn't, things to me the clouds always hid?
You're gone from me now, the way a rainbow disappears
After the sun has erased the clouds in the sky,
And I gaze in awe at the thought somehow,

Nature

That loving rainbows was becoming of you.
You knew where to look for answers to questions in your heart,
You discovered rainbows brought something new.
I now love rainbows, and I can see what you wanted me to see.
That a rainbow is a promise from God,
And we know when it rains, the sun will always return.
Just like a rainbow, you are gone, but, you won't always be.
When I see a rainbow, I will think of you.
Oh, how like it you are with all the colors beautifully in view.
It will tell me when the pain starts to grow,
Like the sun renewing a promise,
Your touch, your presence, I will again know.

Kathleen Hamilton
(Oct.1982)

We all have a story held deep inside
That can reveal a passion
From which we cannot hide,
A passion that tells us who we are,
That can dazzle the spirit
To reach for a star,
Creativity, the essence of The Divine,
Inspires us to let passion be our motive to let our love shine.

Passion and Creativity
Tools to Find Yourself

$\mathcal{CQDC}$

We have a vocation here on earth, one that we agreed upon and knew the value of prior to our arrival. It is to become a co-creator with God—to cherish and appreciate all that is born out of our creations, allowing them to teach us, inspire us, and help us navigate our trials so we may experience our divinity. It is through the spirit of our passions and the act of creating that we discover who we are. Passion is the love that starts the engines of creativity. It is the fire that drives us to search for ourselves and discern who we want to be. Never deny passion or the power to create for it is a God-given endowment. Man is constantly in the act of creating—moment by moment trying to decide through the choices he makes what his passions will manifest.

One cannot deny that God is creative. Just look around, everything you see God has created in all its beauty and splendor. As his image bearers, we too possess the ability to be creative. We are not all the same with our abilities or our desires, and it isn't so much about the finished product of our creations as it is about the act itself. When you experiment with your creativity, you discover what makes you feel good, what makes you happy, and what makes you satisfied. Through trying, you begin to recognize the talents and gifts God specifically endowed you with, the gifts that will contribute to others and the gifts that bring fulfillment.

Being creative connects us to God, and by being connected, we begin to understand who he is, and by understanding that, we begin to understand our creation and purpose. God is the source of all creativity and he gave man the power of creation so he may follow in his path.

How many times have you heard someone moan that they wish they were creative like someone else they knew? Have you ever heard someone say, "I just don't have any talent?" Or "I'd like to be passionate about something, but I'm not." Perhaps they are trying to be inspired by thinking that they must imitate someone else in order to find approval in the act of creating. We doom ourselves to limitations when we settle for the mediocrity of following someone else with whom their talent or achievement was something natural and born within them to feed. We deny our own beauty and wisdom when we believe we have come short of someone else's creativity. We can stand back and admire and even be grateful for world-changing accomplishments, but to deny listening to our own heart or refuse to go it alone, we are living in fear of our own passions.

Imagine what life would be like if men were not inspired to be creative or stayed safely in the shadows of those who were. We would have no cities, no buildings to dwell in, no beautiful gardens or agriculture that gives us wonderful food winter, spring, summer, and fall. We would have no music, no dance, no musical instruments; no computers, no cell phones, and no iPads. Because of fear, we would have nothing that gives our lives pleasure and comfort. Everything we enjoy on this earth is a direct result of someone stepping out of their comfort zone of creativity. Whatever your passion is or whatever you would love to see come into reality within the limitless boundaries of your mind, there will always be someone standing on the sidelines to tell you it is not possible or that you are wrong, yet to stand firm in spite of them and rise to meet the vision of your imagination takes courage. There are very few things in life that do not require courage.

God is the giver of all gifts and he chooses which gifts to give each of his children. We are not all created the same. Some of us have artistic abilities, others musical abilities, and others the ability to craft things with their hands or write words that inspire. Some possess spiritual abilities and talents of discernment and some are given the gift of inventing new ideas. The list goes on and on. Our gifts are part of who we are and we should seek to know and understand what they are and when we do, be grateful for them, and learn how to serve with them.

As a child, I wished I could sing, but believed I couldn't because of the lack of encouragement. Yet I always had a little seed of desire to try. I was given piano lessons, and I struggled with them, but now, the piano gives me a great deal of enjoyment even on a simple level.

When I was twenty-three, I decided to drive home and spend the weekend with my parents, even though I knew they had plans to attend the wedding of my father's boss. It was a casual occasion, so Mom wanted to drag me along to get some visiting in while at the same time, they made their appearance. When we arrived, I noticed a lady playing an organ and singing. I enjoyed things like that, so I convinced my parents to take a seat at the large round table next to the stage where she was performing. Throughout the evening, we were pleasantly entertained with her selection of songs and her interaction with the crowd. I was surprised at how many songs I actually knew. She noticed my interest in her playing and during her break asked if I played. "Not very well," I replied, "but I'm going to start practicing a little more because you've made it look fun." Then, she asked me if I liked to sing and I matter-of-factly declared, "Why, yes of course, doesn't everybody?" Before I knew it, she publically invited me to come up and sing a song. The look on my face was nothing compared to the look on my parents' faces. I didn't have time to think up a good excuse why I couldn't do it before the crowd started to applaud. I had no option but to shove my fear aside—trembling as I was, and get up and sing. I moved closer to her, took the microphone, and turned to see full-blown terror stamped on my parents' faces. My father's eyes looked like they were going pop right out of their sockets. I could just hear his brain ticking away like an antique pocket watch. Tic-tic—what is my crazy daughter up to now? Tic-tic—I could lose my job! Tic-tic—where is the nearest exit so we can make a fast escape?

I sang "Feelings," of course in the wrong key and the wrong tempo and I knew I sounded terrible, but for some reason, I was not embarrassed. My parents were, but I only had to remind myself that I'd probably never have to face anyone in that room again. The real magic was that I felt pleased because in spite of my fear, I did it. That night also burned a desire in me to work at singing until I got better. I also came to the conclusion that if God put a seed of desire in me, then somehow, he knew I was capable of learning how to do it. I signed up for voice courses in our junior college, and throughout the years, I have sung my heart out and have learned to use music and singing for teaching. It has not only brought me joy, but it has been my friend through many tough times. It was worth holding onto the dream, even though I imagined I was not capable of it.

Until one is committed, there is hesitancy, the chance to draw back—concerning all acts of initiative (and creation), there is one elementary truth that ignorance of which kills countless ideas and splendid plans: that the moment one definitely commits oneself, then providence moves too. All sorts of things occur to help one that would never otherwise have occurred. A whole stream of events issues from the decision, raising in one's favor all manner of unforeseen incidents and meetings and material assistance, which no man could have dreamed would have come his way. Whatever you can do, or dream you can do, begin it. Boldness has genius, power, and magic in it. Begin it now.10
— William Hutchinson Murray

Most of us are given more than one talent, and many know it, but there are those who are not aware of what their gifts are. How do they find out? The secret to finding your passion is born mostly out of experience. Discovering your passions for work and for life follows the same route—experience. If you want to discover a fiery passion, put yourself in a position to have a fiery experience. You need to give yourself every opportunity to try something new, read something new, or go somewhere new. I didn't have much experience with horses until I met a man who loved them and asked me to go riding with him. I could love this, I thought and didn't hesitate a minute to go. I enjoyed riding, but realized it would be something that would take a great deal of time to get good at, and I wasn't sure I was passionate enough to dedicate the time, but how was I to know unless I tried? It is by sorting and sifting through new experiences that we discover what excites us. When we try new things, we find out if it is for us by listening to our hearts and paying attention to our life. If we have a desire to know, God will flip on the switch that lightens our hearts to know. It has been said that what we pay attention to is what grows. Hold still long enough to listen to the whispers and to see the signs and recognize the symbols of your gifts. Ask and he will tell you in one of four ways: as a feeling, a thought, an action, or a sense of being. Sometimes, the most difficult part of recognizing your talents is just that, getting a small glimpse of what you are capable of doing. Many people believe that if something doesn't come natural or easy that they are not capable of ever excelling at it. While it may seem like hard work or tedious boredom, it is necessary to master the skill and learn the basics. Exercising your talents also involves discipline.

God will provide the inspiration and it will be your responsibility to act. Part of the creative process is to take the vision or inspiration God gives you and process it .How can being creative help with the grief process? Creativity is life-giving essence and it is hard to exist without it. Nothing of value or greatness has ever been accomplished without passion because anything we do with passion comes from our hearts. When we are grieving, we may feel like the hamster that continually spins the wheel in his cage, going nowhere, accomplishing nothing, and becoming exhausted. Grief can be a creativity blocker that keeps us from discovering, exercising, and recognizing our gifts and talents. Yet it is through the self-discovery of creativity that we can find gratitude, joy, and enlightenment, all of which are conducive to healing. It takes a giant leap of faith to decide to get off the wheel and jump into the arena, but it is necessary for survival. When you begin to know what your passions are, you will be able to create the opportunities that enable you to grow in the right direction and to serve others with your gifts. Throughout our lives, we are a continual unfolding of creativity. We first have an instinct or vision, then a thought or opinion that needs to find a place to take root, then the patience for it to bear fruit. Trust the instinct, desire, or inspiration even though you can render no sane reason why. Life is one large accumulation of experiences. The more you experience, the more passionate you become.

As you think about increasing or finding your passions, remember they are the things you like, the things that make you feel joyful, and the things that excite and fire you up with energy. They make you want to learn more, experience more, and you feel empty without them. Most people can identify with not only one but many passions. You might ask yourself this question: If I was told I only had one week left to live and I could choose to do just one thing and do it well, what would I want to do? Then be excited when you know you don't only have one week, and you don't have to settle for just one.

Self-expression through creativity can teach you to heal. Access your soul to the inner powers you may believe you have forgotten. The power of the soul is passion. It is creativity. It is intuition and they all connect you to The Divine.

Creativity is just connecting things. When you ask creative people how they did something, they feel a little guilty because they didn't really do it, they just saw something. It seemed obvious to them after a while. That's because they were able to connect experiences they've had and synthesize new things. And the reason they were able to do that was that they've had more experiences or they have thought more about their experiences than other people.11
—*Steve Jobs*

Enlightenment can be as simple sometimes as seeing something. Sometimes, we are gifted with awareness when we desire to know and we recognize the truth, the beauty, and sometimes, the obvious. One of the great lessons here is that sometimes the secret to creating something is to just stop and look at things that no one else has bothered to look at.

While we have the gift of life, it seems to me the only tragedy is to allow part of us to die—whether it is our spirit, our creativity or our glorious uniqueness.
—*Gilda Radner*

Sometimes, creativity involves stepping out of our comfort zone and not being afraid to fail. We all have access to the remarkable energies and powers of creativity, but it requires us to let go of uncertainties and negativity and just take it on. When you commit to be creative, you will feel the healing, see the purpose, and bring out the beauty from within.

Think about this for a moment: What will you leave behind when your earth school is completed? Everything we do to express our passion and creativity is Godly. I have boxes of papers and creative artwork that my children created when they were small, and when I hold them in my hands, I feel their warmth. They are small in comparison to the magnitude of the world, but they are a treasure to me, to my heart, and to my memories. They all count. What will you leave, or better yet, what will you be?

A familiar voice, like a summer breeze whispers,
You are not alone,
It whispers truth within your heart,
As if you've always known.
It whispers like a trumpet,
Yet gently shines a light
Through the storm,
Onto the path that you know is right.
You know its truth, you feel the love—
You hear it loud and clear
Be still, and listen, listen, listen
And know that God is near.

Whispers
Tools of Comfort

voice of truth that comes from within can seem as loud as a trumpet sounding victory or a sonic boom because the feeling is undeniable, but most of the time, it is a whisper or a feeling calmly floating like a feather on a gentle breeze. It is within each of us and can become the peace in a storm if we recognize and listen to it.

I call this voice the Comforter or the Holy Ghost. When we hear the Comforter, when we pay attention to what it is telling us, we begin to truly know that we are walking in the light. This spiritual gift is Divine guidance and it helps us drop the fear about our personal welfare, but also the fear we hold inside for our families, our friends, even our nation. It can guide us to know what we as an individual can do to find our port in the storm, our safe mooring in the harbor, and what we can do to help others safely find theirs. It is the switch that turns on the light to our internal truth meter.

People are born with some measure of hearing this whisper, but to truly tap into this consciousness of God's presence is developed by patience and perseverance, but also by a willingness to be quiet and still enough to hear the message. God has said, "Be still and know that I am God."

When I wrote before that God does not expect us to travel grief alone, I literally meant it. When I understood how this "still small voice" was capable of communicating with me, I never felt alone. When anger, hurt, or frustration was so great I believed I couldn't get through it, something would whisper to me that I could and it would prompt me to move in a certain direction. The key was to believe and to trust it.

How exactly do the whispers work? They can give us loving promptings. Promptings take the form of inspirations or urges that show us what to do and sometimes with whom or when. It is tender when it speaks and we can receive the message without having to put up walls of defense. It can help us understand, it can witness truth, it can testify of divinity, and it can soften our hearts and lead us to peace.

Sometimes, we may wish we could hear voices of confirmation when promptings arrive, but God surpasses everyone with nonverbal communication. He speaks very clearly to our souls with inner swelling and feelings of rising energy. Sometimes, it can be so faint yet so strong, leaving no doubt as to the power of the message. Sometimes, we can miss it if we are not paying attention or we are lost in continual bouts of negative energy. When a warm feeling points us in the right direction, it can also give us the energy we need to move in that direction.

Here's what I have learned about listening to promptings: when I heed the impulse burning within me is when I usually witness a miracle. Be cautious not to expect them to take care of trivial decisions we know we are capable of making or by attempting to save ourselves the work of learning and applying lessons of value and responsibility. If we demand with arrogance and unruliness, we can shut the gift out. The spirit will never speak to us in a critical or unloving way. The urgings of the "still small voice" are primarily for pathways to love or healing. After all, God is all about love. We are needed to help him and his angels assist us so we understand how to serve one another. This is why loving whispers can abound in us and God wants them to. They are one of the ways God keeps us connected with each other.

The "still small voice" can teach us. Whispers offer heavenly guidance in the form of insight and understanding along with inspiration. Some who get tangled in hurt from others' negative behaviors are sometimes able to look at things differently when a whisper needs to teach them. They can be taught to change their perception. Whispers teach us where to find the resources to learn or they inspire us to forgive when forgiving is necessary for our well-being.

By listening to the whispers, we can learn to trust our intuition. Sometimes, our intuition can help us know something without being able to explain how we came to the conclusion rationally. It can be the mystery of a gut feeling or what we call instinct that can turn out to be right. When you have tried everything you know and are stuck at a crossroads, getting in touch with your intuition can help. Learning how to listen with your heart can help you develop your intuition and discover how to effectively apply it in your life. God puts into our hearts what we need to know and then whispers it quietly. Practice trusting it.

I had a close friend that came to me for some advice about something that could ultimately end her marriage. She was confused and frustrated, but it was the desire of her heart to do the right thing. I knew of her weary attempt at soul-searching. She had come to a crossroad. She didn't want to upset any apple carts, yet to move in the direction of peace, she might have to.

It was in July and we found ourselves together on a long road trip. Half of the trip was taken talking about her dilemma. I wanted to help, but I couldn't interfere with my opinion, because it was a choice she had to make since it would directly affect her life.

When we came to a rest stop, we decided to pull over and stretch our legs. I was standing on a small patch of grass when I felt a warm breeze move through my hair and across my back. A strong feeling engulfed me, I felt peace and I knew what I had to tell her, and just as I turned, she despairingly walked up beside me. I could tell her problem had robbed her of her energy. "So what is your honest opinion about what I should I do?" she asked, letting out a sigh of frustration. "I just wish God would send a bolt of lightning to give me an answer!"

"But I think you do know the answer," I told her. "I think you're fighting what your heart has been trying to tell you all along. I think you are more afraid of how it might make someone else feel than what is right for your life."

She looked at me with confusion. "I do know?" she asked, holding her hand over her eyes to shield the sun. She appeared confused, as if I had known all along but only then decided to give my opinion.

"When you think about what someone else is asking of you versus what you want, how do you feel?" I asked her to stop and think for a few minutes, and then asked again. "What is the feeling you get in your gut when you think about what you must do to please and keep peace versus what your heart tells you?"

"I feel dark, I feel scared, and I feel like I am sinking in quicksand, and I am angry!" she replied with certainty.

"There's your answer," I said. "When you are doing the right thing, God whispers peace, he whispers love, and by those fruits, we know what is right."

She thought a moment, lifted her head high, stood as straight as a soldier, and said she felt like the weight of the world had just been lifted off her shoulders. She admitted she really knew in her heart what she had to do, but it wasn't going to be easy—but she invariably did it anyway.

Sometimes, we find ourselves in so much turmoil that we become deaf and blind to heaven's messages. If you keep chasing for answers and straining too hard to hear, they will elude you. Let the answer, like the warm breeze on that July day, come gently. Ponder and allow the message to be received and learn to trust that God cares and is guiding you. When you begin to trust, you will get better at tuning in, and when you tune in, your inner confidence will grow. Learn how to meditate, go to that silent place to have a one-on-one time with your Maker. You will get better at hearing if you do.

A couple of weeks before Lanette's death, I experienced my first over-powering whisper. It came with enough force to literally keep me glued in place until I understood it. I had spent a typical day cleaning house, doing the laundry, and trying to tie loose ends together before it was time to make dinner and call it a day. I was holding a load of clothes that were headed for the shelves in my bedroom closet when I decided to stop at Lanette's room and ask her to grab the other basket in the laundry room and put the things away for me. As was typical for a preteen who believed her mother was out to make her life miserable, she snapped back that she didn't feel like doing it at the moment. I was annoyed at her response and stepped into her room, ready to ground her from something so she would realize that, in spite of what she thought, I really didn't ask much of her in the first place. "Some of those clothes are yours!" I snapped. "Should I just leave them in there until you need something to wear or throw them back in the dirty clothes hamper?" I was agitated, so I decided to put my things away before dealing with her any further. "I will be back in a minute to finish this conversation," I warned as I gave her the evil eye and headed for my room.

I stepped into my closet, becoming more irritated as I attempted to arrange my things on the shelf. She was becoming hard to handle; attempts at discipline or any kind of parental interaction usually turned into a power struggle. I let out a sigh of frustration as I continued to wonder how I was going to drive my point home about her being willing to pitch in and help once in a while. "How am I going to get through her hard head?" I mumbled as I tossed a stack of clothes on the top shelf. They no sooner landed in a perfectly stacked pile when I was prompted to stand still—not move. I lowered my arms, but again, I was prompted to stand still. "Do nothing," the whisper said. "Do nothing." I moved, but again, the whisper came. "Stand still." Finally, I stood frozen in place. After a moment passed, I was told: "Do nothing, all this will pass before you know it, and you and Lanette will be okay. Do nothing but tell her you love her, you will be grateful you did."

I dropped my arms, and I started to leave the closet, wondering how doing nothing would only teach her to be more disrespectful. If I let it go, she'll get worse, I thought. Again, as if two hands where placed on my shoulders to command stillness, the message came again word for word. I guess I was a slow learner, or just stubborn, but I finally held still long enough to think about the prompting and how strong it hit me, and I knew I had to follow it. To this day, I am eternally grateful that I did.

When I thought about that powerful moment in the closet and the powerful message it delivered, I am amazed at the wisdom it provided, not only for the peace of the following two weeks, but for the realization that God knew her days on the earth were limited and he was giving me a few more unencumbered moments with her—moments with no regrets.

Having a quiet mind is a good place to start if you want to develop the ability to listen to the whispers when they come. Quiet is needed at first to be able to clearly distinguish your thoughts from the mind or the spirit.

Once you determine which is which, you can tune into them way more often. As I said, mediation is a start. It is nothing more than quieting the mind. Simply sit quietly for a few minutes a day. If your mind is chattering away on what seems like endless chitchat, don't worry, it will quiet down. Work toward the goal of just being still. The more you do it, the easier it becomes.

When you become aware of the spirit world that surrounds you and you learn to listen to the flow of wisdom directed your way, you will realize how the hosts of heaven and your loved ones are closer than you think. We are not alone, we never were, and we never will be. That is what the whispers impart to me. I embrace it and always welcome it. When I am blessed with a whisper, I am usually blessed with a miracle.

Journal:

On Monday evening at Lanette's viewing, a woman handed me a note that was handwritten on a torn piece of notebook paper. Even though I had seen her at church, I did not know her personally. Her name was Betty and she was awakened Saturday morning with a prompting to write something down on a piece of paper and she did not know why. She had not heard about Lanette's accident, but the prompting to get up and write down the message that was being given to her was so strong she knew not to ignore it. That afternoon, she was telling a mutual friend about it and said she was still confused who the message was for. Our friend was shaken and told Betty she knew exactly who it was meant for. She asked Betty to go to the viewing or the funeral and give the note to me because she knew the message was from Lanette. They talked about it more, and both agreed that I was probably too overcome with grief to receive the message myself. Even though I felt Lanette had given me a message the night she died, I understood that when someone is so overcome with the pain and shock of suddenly losing someone, they can only absorb so much information, so, many times, God uses other people to deliver messages.

Whispers

The Heavenly Message:
Mama and Daddy,
Please don't weep for me, for the treasures of heaven are greater, you see,
than all of earth's riches and fame were for me. So, Mama, dear Mama,
don't weep for me. A marriage eternal I'll not be denied, for my Father in
heaven will place by my side a vessel that's worthy—oh, can't you see?
Nothing—my Father will keep back from me.

Journal:
November 8, 1982
> *Today, I went into Lanette's room and looked at all the things she*
> *cherished while here and thought about how important some of them*
> *were to her—only to be left behind. The first night after I got home from*
> *the hospital, I picked up her shoes and cried knowing how she loved them.*
> *She worked hard for them and was proud she bought them with her own*
> *money. I felt sad that she would never wear them again. I couldn't bear*
> *to look at or touch her clothes because she would never wear them again.*
> *I had to leave the room, the sadness was too overpowering.*
>
> *A few days later, I went back into her room and picked up her shoes*
> *again. On that day, I felt peace because I sensed Lanette was there with*
> *me. I heard a whisper say, "None of those things matter to me anymore,*
> *Mom. If you only knew what I know, you would understand that I now*
> *know where to place value on things that are important." I suddenly*
> *understood what was meant when the scriptures tell us to lay up our*
> *treasures in heaven and not on earth because the things that really do*
> *matter are those things that are spiritual and not material.*

You can hear the voice of heaven if you choose to. You can hear the
whispers; just remember they are very delicate. Whispers are fine spiritual
communications and are not familiar to our physical eyes or our physical ears, but they are familiar to our spirit. Spiritual knowledge cannot
be communicated with words alone. When we receive the message, we
feel it within ourselves and say with certainty, "This I understand! "The
voice of the Spirit is neither harsh nor loud, but rather as a still and small

voice of perfect mildness. Yet it can pierce the soul and cause the heart to burn. Occasionally, the whisper will press firmly enough to help us pay attention, as it did with me in the closet, but usually, if we do not heed the gentle prompting or if we do not listen with our feelings, it will withdraw and wait—wait for us.

Like sunlight filtering through a cloudy sky
Angels hover consciously by,
They wait for an invitation to serve our needs,
And rejoice in spirit when they see our good deeds.
They listen with joy when we laugh or sing,
And in our sorrow, comfort they desire to bring.
As we attempt to walk in the light,
They are there by our side.
To serve, protect, and gently guide.

Angels
A Tool of Light

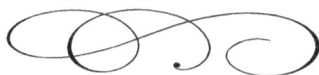

O ut of curiosity, I began asking people what they thought about angels. One woman said, "I don't think of them much, probably because they seem more like a fantasy than a reality."

Another man said, "Sure, I believe there are angels everywhere—good ones and bad ones."

Another question I asked: "Do you believe we each have angels around us to protect us?"

One woman answered, "Well, maybe some do, but I don't recall them showing up in my life."

If someone would have asked me either one of those questions when I was eighteen, I might have answered: Yes, I've heard stories of angels, but personally, I haven't had proof they are around me. Now, however, living through grief and asking the powers of heaven to rescue me more than once, I must say I know they are real and I know they are available every hour of every day.

Many people believe in angels in one way or another, their concepts may differ, but few actually acknowledge that they have a burning testimony in their hearts for knowing about them on a personal level.

I was trying to finish my shopping one summer day in time to get home and prepare for a gathering we were hosting. I was scurrying in and out of different stores, trying to check off a list of things I needed. Coming out of the last store, I realized I was running about thirty minutes late. I hated feeling rushed—it was such a stressor. Hurried thoughts were running through my mind as I tried to make a beeline to the car, but I came to an abrupt stop when I felt a hand on my shoulder. I twisted around to stare into the eyes of a tall young man who appeared unstable and ready to ask me for something. I was alarmed he had gotten close enough to touch me without being aware of his presence. I assumed he was an intoxicated panhandler who probably wanted money for alcohol. It was a strange moment for me because I felt locked in time. Only a suspension of time could have processed all the thoughts and questions that coursed through my mind.

I stopped, stared deeply into a pair of glazed blue eyes. I felt a strange connection with him, but didn't know why. Yet only a heartbeat later, I visualized my son standing there. My heart ached. For years, I had powerlessly observed him wage his war on despair and alcoholism. The young man standing before me could so easily have been him. My compassion arose, and for a split second, I felt a yearning to rescue him. I asked myself what I was going to do if he asked me for money. I easily assumed he'd probably buy alcohol with it. I stopped giving my son money for that reason. Instantly, my mind jumped to another concern—should I offer to buy him food? Maybe he was hungry or maybe he needed to know someone cares. Miraculously, I not only had all these questions parade through my mind in the small moment that this encounter lasted, but I also had time to process them.

However, a question from this young man never came. When our eyes locked long enough to look past the physical, he took his hand off my shoulder, lowered his head, and whispered, "Thank you," and moved away.

I wanted to scream, "Wait!" But he was gone. I walked to my car in a trance, shaking and wondering what he had seen in my eyes that prompted him to turn away in the humble reverent manner he did. Did he see love? Did he see compassion? Did he feel non-judged or maybe ashamed, shy, or too embarrassed to ask what he had stopped me to ask?

I drove home slowly, reflecting on what had just happened and why it had affected me so deeply. Before I arrived home I came to the conclusion that it was no accident or coincidence that the young man reached out and stopped me or that I didn't see him approach. He appeared for a reason. He had a message.

Angels

I had prayed so many times on behalf of my son, and what I saw outside that store others would probably have judged as a drunken bum, a menace to society, or a worthless panhandler, yet I a saw a young man, a child of God, a person much like my son, put on this earth and desperately struggling to find his way. I looked at him with compassion just as I would want someone to look at my son if he was the one standing there. By the time I arrived home, the message was clear. Don't give up on your son— just love him. God hears your prayers. The truth of the message resonated with me and I wept.

I couldn't stop thinking and wondered if I had seen an angel—sent to me to tell me to not give up or if I was an angel to this young man. Maybe he needed to look into the eyes of someone that didn't judge his value. For all I know, he might have gone home that day and decided to change the course of his life. Sometimes, that's how God uses people: he sends angels to prompt them to do something that can have an impact on someone else's life. Yet for me, I saw an angel that day. When we exchanged looks, I was touched by his spirit. Whether it came in a physical manner or a spiritual one, I got the message.

When I was young, I asked my mother if God could be everywhere at once.

"I don't know," she replied, "but I know his influence can be, and I know he has many helpers."

Then I had the same question about Santa Claus. If God can't be everywhere at once, then how does Santa cover the world in one night? He certainly is not smarter than God. How can he be in the downtown mall on Saturday night when I heard he was going to be in the valley mall on Saturday night? Are they his influences? Or are they his helpers?

"Santa can't do it without many helpers," was Mom's definite reply.

Children don't hesitate to ask the questions that just don't make sense. Many times, innocent questions launch searches and searches lead to more questions and more questions solve mysteries. By the time we are grown, most of us have solved the Santa Claus mystery, but have we solved the mystery about God and his large sphere of influence and his helpers? Can God be everywhere at once? Of course, but he also has helpers.

I believe in angels! They are real; they exist and have a purpose in our lives. The idea of calling on angels can seem like a mysterious phenomenon or fantasy, but nothing could be further from the truth. If you actually think about it, human life could fall into the category of mysterious phenomena, but of course, we know we are real. We have talked about the fact that just because you can't see God doesn't mean he doesn't exist, so it is with angels. Angels are not physical beings, they are spiritual. Jesus once said to Nicodemus: "Just as you can hear the wind but can't tell where it comes from or where it will go next, so it is with the Spirit."

Angels are mentioned over one hundred times in the Old Testament and over one hundred and sixty times in the New Testament. It shows that man has been aware of them for a long time. An angel's mission is love; they are messengers, guides, supporters, encouragers, calming mediators, and teachers who will gladly come to your aide with a simple thoughtful request.

Betty J. Eadie in her book, *Embraced by the Light,* tells of watching angels hovering above the people on earth. She said the angels knew each one by name and watched over them closely. Their purpose was to be there to help give direction and protection and that we could call on them to come to our aid if we ask in faith. Can you imagine the kind of loving God that would make available to his children this kind of loving help and direction if we just have the faith to ask for it? When you have a thought, the vibration of that thought immediately calls forth the attention of your spiritual supporters. That is why it has often been said that our thoughts are responsible for creating our life. And when your thoughts come from a place of love that is when you find an angel by your side.

It is difficult enough to come to this earth with a veil over our memory of our preexistence with God and try to stumble our way through life, but imagine trying to struggle our way through pain, sorrows, and mistakes and learn love and compassion without some form of help or guidance.

Besides being messengers and supporters, angels deliver warnings. They issue proclamations and interpret dreams and visions, all of which are instruments in carrying out God's will on earth. They are particularly knowledgeable in the sequence of events, not only can they warn of impending danger, but they also are knowledgeable of things which have not yet come to pass.

Just as I was instructed to stand still in the closet, I believe it was an angel telling me to do so, but my strong will wasn't quite so willing to embrace it at first, so I also believe it was the voice of the Comforter that witnessed I was hearing truth. God knew Lanette's time with me would soon be ending, and the angels were there to impart the love and the ways to help me understand. My lessons, however, did not arrive all at once. Time and thoughtful contemplation and other encounters brought me to a state of knowing. It would be nice if lessons could come quick and easy, but there is wisdom in knowing that some don't.

Does God, Jesus, or any of his devout servants ever interact with us one on one? Absolutely! And many times throughout history, they have, but angels are given a very powerful and influential job as well. God uses them to communicate with his earthly children. Sometimes, the messages are delivered to a single human and, sometimes, to multitudes. Sometimes, the message may be a warning and, sometimes, a bearer of good news.

Another job angels are given is to comfort those who are grieving, going through trials, or suffering. They also help protect our children. I used to hear that the prayers of mothers were powerful prayers because the pure love of a mother is like the kind of love God has for all his earthly children.

So then the question might arise: Where was the protection when my child died? I can only say that eventually, death will come to us all. I was led to understand that in her case, it was her appointed time to go. Yes, many tears had to flow before that understanding, but many times since, I have been able to tap into the comfort and be guided through the tough times. Of course, the sting of losing a loved one is always difficult, but there are also many other times in life, other than death, that can drop us to our knees or cause suffering and we should not hesitate to ask for help through those as well.

How do you call on your angels? It is simple—just summons them either in your thoughts or a voiced prayer, it doesn't matter. It's all personal preference how you choose to ask. If you open up to the energy, you will feel their presence. There are times I feel discouraged or I feel fearful and I ask for angels to touch my heart to feel peace, and it doesn't take very long before I know they have done their work or guided me to know what to do. Some pleas have been a simple, "Please send me angels because I do not know what to do."

There are many kinds of angels that serve different purposes in our lives, but we don't have to understand each one in order to begin asking for the right one. We are never alone. Knowing that can bring us comfort during difficult times and ignite hope when we are afraid. Some angel's presence may feel stronger when we are in danger or when we require spiritual help, yet at any time we ask for advice or understanding, they hear. They have the wisdom to know what you need.

There are times angels enlist the help of other people to help you. Or you may be asked to be a miracle in someone else's life. Angels feel blessed to serve us because they understand the rewards of service and they want to help us understand as well.

One of the most difficult things we humans have to learn to embrace is asking for help and trusting in our Heavenly Father's love and grace. When we trust before we ask for divine help, it is there the minute we utter the plea. God wants us to understand that our life has meaning and our life has value and there is a purpose for us being here. He doesn't want us to feel poor, be afraid, depressed, unlucky, or alone. Anyone who teaches differently is not delivering God's message.

I recall the time I attended The Compassionate Friends support group and was sharing a story about a spiritual experience that had taken place the week before when a man loudly interrupted me and said, "I think those kind of things are all wishful thinking on your part. We want to believe, so we make up stories that make us feel good."

Gratefully, what he said didn't upset me and all I could reply was: "Only the person who experiences such things truly knows it is what it is. I hope someday you can personally understand the truth of what I say, but it will come through your experience."

At that time, I was still new to everything, but I had begun to trust in my ability to discern the difference between wishful thinking and spiritual experiences. It was and always has been a work in progress.

When my parent's three younger children were still at home, they decided to take a trip to the Northwest to visit relatives. While there, they decided to take the kids to a secluded beach where they could romp in the sand and soak up sunshine. My two brothers were digging around a large boulder that had probably sat on that beach for years and the older of the two disturbed the sand under it enough to make it shift. Before he had a chance to move, he was pinned down and could feel it slowly overcoming him. He was on his knees with his hands trying to push it away, but soon realized he was no match. Without a miracle, he knew he was going to be crushed to death.

My other brother went screaming for my father, and panic set in because one man or even two was no match for the boulder. My brother, about sixteen at the time, said that even though he knew he was in trouble, something told him to hold perfectly still, and if he did, he would be safe. He realized it was like dealing with quicksand—the more you fight, the faster you go down.

"I knew I had to listen," he said, "for that is how I would survive, so I held perfectly still."

Miraculously, my father scraped up about twenty-five men out of nowhere and they ran to his aide. Even then, without Divine help, they were no match. They uttered a prayer, held the rock long enough for someone to pull my brother out, and when they moved away, the large boulder tumbled a couple of times and came to a rest. Without a doubt, my brother would have been crushed had he not held still long enough for help to arrive. I asked him if he believed in angels. "Yes, of course!" he said. "I'm sure it was angels who told me to hold still."

The more these things appear in your life, the more accepting and grateful you become of their reality.

I took a trip once to visit some friends who lived in a small town in eastern Oregon. I took the shortest route, which took me inland to desolate barren country where there was no cell phone reception. The roads were narrow and surrounded by deep jagged crevices. I remember thinking that if I ran off the road; no one would ever find me.

Dusk was arriving, and I happened to recall my sister telling me that she didn't like being on roads at dusk or dawn because that is when the deer were usually out. The thought of her telling me that had no sooner left my mind when another thought told me to slow down because there were deer on the road ahead. I believed deer only lived where there were trees, grass, and foliage, and there wasn't any of that around. It was just brown, rocky, dry, and desolate, but I knew better than to ignore the warning. I had barely slowed down to a crawl when I rounded a curve, and there, smack dab in the middle of the road stood three large deer staring at me like I had just crashed their party. They had no intention of moving. I gradually eased them out of the way with my car and continued to drive.

The whisper came again. "You are not out of the woods, there are more deer ahead." Again rounding another curve, I came upon two more in the middle of the road. I finally resigned myself to the fact that for the remainder of the drive, desolate wilderness or not, I was going to travel at the speed of a snail. I encountered deer for a third time and was very humble and grateful that I was being watched over. I didn't fail to say "thank you." Angels love to hear that. Well, don't we all?

If you would like to recognize the healing presence of angels, please ask them to make themselves known to you. If you need their comfort but are hesitant to ask for understanding—ask anyway. Ask for the faith to ask.

God wants the desires of our hearts to be fulfilled. Do you need help making a decision, do you long for better relationships, do you want a better job, better finances, or is peace and hope something you long for? Ask. God and his angels are waiting and hoping you will.

I have oftentimes asked the angels to take a message to my child and my mother just in case they are not close by, and I do believe they get the messages.

Remember the corn maze? It's true, life is like a maze and God and his angels are hovering above. They know the big picture. Sometimes when we ask why something is the way it is it might also help to ask, "What is the bigger picture?" There's always a bigger picture.

The best way I know how to invite angels into your life is by being one in someone else's life. This world is in so much need of the love and service we mortal angels can give. When you feel the nudge to reach out or the prompting to do something nice or the encouragement to help someone carry their heavy load, you are opening up your heart to understand your angels. By doing so, your angels will appear and help you do it—you've got my word.

If I were an angel on your shoulder,
I would gently whisper, remember me.
When you see things I love, like rainbows, sunshine
And smiles on faces of those we know, remember me.
Let stars and sunsets that make the horizon glow,
remind you of me.
When you see daisies and roses kissed by the dew,
Don't forget to think of the times I shared them with you.
Listen and hear the melodies of songs that awakened our soul,
It will remind you to remember love is our ultimate goal.
Oh, remember me and smile with pride,
For I remember you and I am waiting,
Holding your heart in my hands, patiently,
Lovingly on the other side.

Reunion
A Tool of Truth

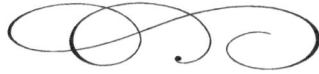

very time a loved one, family member, or friend has returned to the
spirit world, the magnet that draws us in that direction becomes a
little stronger. It is because love is greater than death. Everything
on this physical earth is temporary, but the love that we create and the
love that nourishes us is eternal, imperishable, and indestructible. Earth is
merely our school away from home.

If you can accept the fact that there is life after death, then death loses
its sting. Understanding that those that go before us have simply traveled
to a different place where they wait to reunite with us. Knowing that gives
us reason to live with greater optimism. No one departing this life has lost
more than he has increased. We all take back the valuable earthly lessons.
That is why the longer we can stay here, the more wisdom we attain.

Truth witnesses that nothing separates us from our loved ones forever.
While they wait, they are enthusiastically engaged in good things, enfold-
ed in love, and they know that their leaving earth only means that you do
not have the power to see them with your physical eyes or hear them with
your physical ears. Our ties of love are eternal. They are at peace because
they have knowledge of the bigger picture. They are content to know that
everyone will eventually come to this knowledge. They also know how
valuable earthly existence is for spiritual progression.

Is there a heaven and a hell? Absolutely—for me, hell would be regret—the regret of realizing that I wasted opportunities to grow and to
show more love, compassion, and forgiveness. Those aren't so easy to
achieve. For many of us, it takes a lot of time. Yet because a kind loving
God doesn't want to be separated from his children nor does he desire any
of them to perish, he is always giving us chances to progress so we can

return. That is why growing and obtaining knowledge never ceases—we just advance better here in this life when there is opposition present.

Think about it for a minute--- if this earth is our temporary home, would we be uncomfortable or feel out of place in our real home? What or where is heaven actually? Is heaven our final destination when all is said and done and judgment is rendered? I only know that it doesn't matter if I believe God is a fair and loving God. However, if the meek are to inherit the earth, as Jesus said in Matthew 5:5, then it would make sense to believe that earth was ordained to be our home and we never leave it. So where do the spirits go when they die? The spirit world is here on this planet. The planet has different spheres: one is temporal and the other spiritual. The temporal earth is populated by people with physical bodies, and the other is populated by people with spiritual bodies. When someone lays down their physical body, where do they go? They go into the spiritual realm which is here. Do we all go there? Yes!—the good and the bad. Just as it is here, many kinds of people good and evil occupy this sphere—yet it is my guess that they are very much separated by their deeds. They do not go up into the sky, float around on clouds, or go to the sun or beyond the boundaries of this organized universe. We are brought forth upon this earth for the purpose of inhabiting it for all of eternity. The ultimate goal is to occupy an earth that has been cleansed and populated with those who have learned to love and can live in peace and harmony.

We will be reunited not only with our loved ones, but with those that we knew before as well. We probably have more friends on the other side than we can imagine, and they will meet us more joyfully than we were ever welcomed when we arrived here. There will be many opportunities for close relationships with everyone that we desire to be close to. We will not lose our individuality. We will be ourselves and be recognized as such.

There is great wisdom in not being given too much knowledge concerning the spiritual sphere. To know too much would interfere with the purpose for which our probation on earth was designed. It could no doubt condemn us to a life of misery and ruin by making us content to waste our very valuable education here and slow our progression. God is doubtless more kind to us than we understand by placing a veil over our memory. Yet even when we die, we are still students of a kind and loving God.

My son, Bryan, was nine months old when his sister died. She was like his second mommy; he loved her and was very attached to her. She would style his hair, hold on to him tight, and smother him with kisses. She was helping him learn to walk by holding out her arms and beckoning him to come to her. Whenever he would see her, he would hold out his hands, wiggle his fingers, and cry, "Nett!" It was the name he joyfully voiced when his sister was in sight.

My father was holding him as the family stood beside her casket saying our good-byes. Bryan became agitated and stretched his arms above the casket and began wiggling his fingers saying, "Nett, Nett."

We all looked at each other as his squeals became more determined for his sister to pick him up. We looked up where he had directed his attention and knew he was seeing his sister. He was not looking "down" into her casket. My father sat him on the floor and we watched as he crawled to the head of the casket and again reached up and cried, "Nett, Nett." For a moment, our tears ceased and we knew she was there and aware of our outpouring of love. It would have been impossible to convince us of anything different. The peace we felt was unearthly.

Because of the purity in the hearts of small children and babies, they are able to witness spiritual things that older people miss. In order to live by faith and experience earth life, however, their veil of memory is gradually closed and they usually forget. It is only fair to them that this should be so because it is part of the plan of learning through earthly progression. However, what I found to be so amazing was the weeks after Lanette's death; Bryan became the anchor in my grief because his temperament was so mild and loving. He was content to let me hold him for however long I needed, and I needed to hold him close to me more than ever. He would go to bed without fussing and he would wake in the morning patiently waiting for me to pick him up. I often say that his total acceptance of my needs helped save my life. When I look back on that time, I know that he was being tutored by angels. He was just a baby, but his wisdom was that of a full-grown soul. There are times, however, that older children need comfort from the other side to help them get through the beginning stages of grief. That is what I believe happened to my daughter, Kristy. She was nine at the time her sister died, yet she seemed to be handling things well considering how I was falling apart. I feared she was in denial, and it might hit her hard when the reality set in. One morning while my sister, Sandy, was visiting, we were busy talking and preparing breakfast when Kristy came in and sat down at the kitchen table. She sat for a minute and then began to comment on how Lanette was reading her stories during the night. In perfect sync, Sandy and I made an about-face, glared at her, and scooted over to the table and sat down. Nothing mattered except what Kristy had to say.

"Stories?" I asked. "Lanette is reading you stories?"

"Yeah, she comes into my bedroom and reads me stories about what it is like where she is. She is not standing on the ground though, she is up above me." She leaned over and held her hand about three feet above the floor. "Like this much," she said.

"Are you sure it is Lanette?" I asked in suspense, trusting that she wasn't just trying to be amusing or purposely trying to shake us up.

"Silly," she laughed, "of course it is. Who else would it be?"

"What was she wearing?" I impatiently cross-examined, desiring an answer before I was even through with the question. "She was wearing white," she answered. "But she did have a gold belt on." She added, calmly picking up a slice of toast and taking a bite.

"Wearing white like an angel?" I asked, surely thinking that someone had told her angels wear white. Then I recalled when we put on a play about the "Littlest Angel" and both kids wore white with a gold belt.

"No," she said emphatically. "She is Lanette, not an angel. She looked pretty though, and her shoes looked like her Vans."

Sandy and I looked at each other in amazement. We both knew Lanette's favorite shoes were her three pairs of Vans. "I haven't talked with her about spirits or anything," I said. "She is not getting this from me."

Paying no attention to our conversation, Kristy kept talking.

"She told me she wasn't mad at me anymore because I tattled on her." She smiled like it was a relief that she had been forgiven. "She said that if

I thought the cherries were good here I should taste how sweet they are there. She said food tastes so much better." Kristy looked up, "Why do you think it does, Mom?"

"Maybe because the growing conditions are perfect," I guessed, trying to picture a big luscious cherry oozing with sweet ripe juice.

"I asked Lanette why you had to cry so much," Kristy said, finally directing all her attention toward me and waiting for a response.

"What did she say?" I asked, feeling butterflies in my stomach, yet feeling euphoric as I tried to visualize Lanette in her room conversing with her.

"Lanette said you would be okay, Mom. So don't be so sad—okay?"

Those encounters with her sister got her through the first couple of months, but her memories were gradually phased out. When she was older, I asked her if she remembered any of those things she shared with us, and she said vaguely but that much of it had faded. She did remember the gold belt though and that the shoes she was wearing were Vans. I thought it was amazing that the details weren't forever etched in her memory because of the amount of comfort it gave us adults. It was one of many other faith-building experiences that were still yet to come that testified that all is well with those that die. It is certainly not the end.

The day Lanette died, I came home from the hospital tired, weary, and remorsefully hopeless. I collapsed on the living room sofa and didn't budge for hours. What now? I remember asking. How am I supposed to get through this? I glanced at the chandelier above the dining room table. The kids and I used to say that the five lights in the chandelier represented each one of us in the family. I noticed one of the lights had burned out. I was numb with grief.

As I sat and waited for my mother and father to arrive, a million thoughts ran through my mind like a runaway train. I was angry at Lanette. Why wasn't she careful? Then I felt like a deserter. How could I leave my child at the hospital and just come home? I felt guilty—who was taking care of her body, and were they treating it with respect? Who takes the dead out of the hospital? Whoever it is, do they know she is precious? Do they understand what I lost? Exhaustion set in as I just kept asking myself over and over—what kind of mother would leave her child at the hospital. What was she thinking, feeling, or doing while her body lay alone in the hospital morgue covered with a sheet? Panic began to rise in me the sadder my thoughts became.

Then, like a quiet trumpet announcing the arrival of royalty, I felt my attention drawn to the landing above our sunken living room. I felt two beings standing in front of the spinet piano that set against the wall. I knew one of them was Lanette. How did I know that? A mother knows her child. I knew she was with someone—I felt it was a man and peace engulfed me to realize she was not at the hospital hovering over her body and afraid. I quickly came to understand that the person with her met her when her spirit left her body. I imagined she knew him before she came to earth and I believed she was happy and at peace. For that exhausting and numbing time while I was still in a state of shock, I did feel some comfort just knowing she was not alone. I felt her spirit speak to me. She disclosed that she still had a brother and sister that were waiting to join our family. I looked over to the chandelier, thinking for a split second that there weren't enough lights on the chandelier, and besides, I had given up having more children. A couple of miscarriages had discouraged me.

One month before the first anniversary of Lanette's death, I gave birth to another little sister. A couple months prior to her delivery, I had been wrestling with what I was going to name her when a book sitting on the top shelf in Bryan's closet caught my eye. I was compelled to get it down, and when I did, I noticed a white envelope sticking out from between the pages. Curious, I opened a letter Lanette had written to her grandmother but never mailed. It read:

Dear Grandma,

I am excited that my mother is going to have a baby. I hope she lets me help name it. Here is what I want. If it is a girl, I would like to call her Carrie Lynn. If it is a boy, I would like to name him Jeremy. Knowing Mom, though, she will probably name it whatever she wants.

Reunion

Needless to say, I now have a Carrie Lynn, and the baby boy I lost was Jeremy. I believe Jeremy needed to come to earth long enough to get a body and then God had other plans for him—as it probably is with other babies that die before they have a chance to live.

I don't need to question who placed the letter where I could see it when the time was right—maybe an angel—I don't know, but it doesn't matter because I knew it happened when it needed to happen and I paid attention.

Why do some people live until they are a ripe old age and others die when they are very young? If we have an appointed time to stay, is it fair that someone can take another person's life? Does it alter the plan God has for them? Do all the evil people get the same chance that the good ones do? Does God punish some people and not others? If we try to figure out why all the things happen as they do, we can drive ourselves crazy. Many times, we have to learn how to live and accept that everyone has their free agency, and some do not use it very wisely. However, our souls long for the light, and when we open up our hearts to receive it, we begin to have faith that God knows what he is doing, and sometimes, he lets us in on enough knowledge to give us peace. Our minds are programmed with a yearning to know and learn of eternal things. Our inner work is private and our nature is to desire to be comforted and be assured that our loved ones are okay.

Journal:

Last night, Sandy called me to tell me of her friend, Cindy's, experience. I have known Cindy for some time and know her to be a very loving and compassionate lady, so when she relayed her story to Sandy, I listened with an open heart.

Cindy was driving home from somewhere and she came to an intersection, and thinking it was safe, she proceeded to accelerate through it without seeing a man who stepped out in front of her car. She said she should have hit him except for the fact that just as she stepped on the gas, her car suddenly quit. It wasn't until the engine stopped that she noticed the man, and he yelled at her, "You almost hit me, lady!" She sat there for a second and realized that God had intervened and saved this man's life. Her car had never stalled on her like that before. She then said she thought about Lanette and how easily God could have intervened, but he didn't because the spirit whispered to her that it was her time to go. I am always comforted by these stories, yet I know they don't always alleviate the pain. Maybe it will take time.

Whether someone dies when they are old or young, they are still a spirit with a soul and they see and are aware of what they left here. They do not want us to suffer and become stagnated in our grief to the point that we cannot function in a healthy manner. Until they know that we will be okay, they have a difficult time doing what they need to do on the other side. Many times, they stay close by so we can feel their presence and know they are okay, but at some point, they would like to be involved in other things. They know they will see us again. I'd like to believe that Lanette is a teacher. Even when they are doing things they love to do, they are still aware of our lives, and they still feel our love when we express it and they get our messages when we send them. One of the most loving things we can do to free them is to do something kind or loving for someone else in honor of their memory. Our pain then becomes a tool to freedom rather than a weapon to keep us imprisoned in grief.

We aren't expected to remove them from our minds either. As we travel our journey here, it is still important to remember them and hold their memories close to our hearts as we gather to celebrate traditions or happy events. Memories are a gift. They may not be here physically, but during special times, they are here spiritually. I used to gather my children on Lanette's birthday, bake a cake, and we would reminisce about some of our happy memories of her. It brought us comfort to do that. Do I bake a cake every year for her now? No, but I don't bake one every year for my other children either, however, I do think about them, or give them a call to wish them happy birthday. If we do get together, everyone is usually trying to leave sugar alone, so we don't always have cake, but we have each other.

Yet in the beginning, it was an important ritual for the family because it helped bring her closer to us, especially for the kids.

There are times people have the opportunity to say good-bye and there are times they don't; it's more about us having the opportunity to express our feelings, but for the ones who have left, they don't hold on to the disappointment if the chance didn't exist, because they know and understand how we feel. I was blessed to be able to converse with my mother right up to an hour before she died. I didn't want to beat around the bush and avoid saying the "D" word because it was important that I let her know a few things. I told her I loved her and that I would be there for my father and I asked her to let Lanette know that she is very much missed and remembered. However, those were all the things I used to say to her before she came close to death. Each day we live, we have the opportunity to express love so there will be no regrets.

When I asked my mother to pass my message on, she just smiled and weakly whispered, "I'm sure she knows that already, but I will tell her anyway." I had a little envy for my mother because I knew it wouldn't be long until she could look into my child's eyes, see her smile, and feel her arms around her again. I knew she missed her almost as much as I did.

Sometimes, one of the most frequent requests from people that know they are going to die is to not forget them. As I thought about that, I thought about all the things that made my daughter and mother unique and precious, and I think of them often. I remember Lanette when I see a rainbow or mashed potatoes, gravy, and biscuits. Whenever we would eat out, she would order something with mashed potatoes and gravy because she loved to dip her biscuits in the gravy. She loved to play school. Many times, she would spend whatever money she could get to buy paper, pens, and crayons for her students. She dreamed of being a teacher. I remember her giggle. I remember how well she sang her ABCs when she was only fifteen months old. When I see patent leather shoes, I think of her wearing her little white Mary Jane's and placing them on her pillow when she went to bed. I remember conversations with my mother, and those moments when she would stop everything to teach me a mini lesson. I was complaining once about one of our alcoholic relatives staying with us too long, and Mom put her finger up to her lips and whispered for me to be quiet, then said: "Remember, when you do it unto the least of these, you do it unto me." I knew she was quoting Jesus and I got the message. The memories go on and on, and I smile.

No one on the other side wants their death to diminish anyone's life. I often feel that when it is my time to go, I would like to leave this world just a little bit better than when I came. I don't want people to feel sad when they think of me. I would like to be remembered as a person who discovered her specific reason or mission for being here and magnified it with value and love. I would like to be remembered as someone who radiated light, yet I know that becoming that way takes ongoing experiences that require one's full heart. It is not something that can be attained with only our five physical senses.

If you can look at the beautiful things in nature that God has created for us, would you think he would give any less for those who have gone to the other side? I am sure the trees are greener, the fruit sweeter, the rivers clearer, and the flowers and their colors more vibrant. Just think of the beauty that must surround them!

If you can embrace the idea of a beautiful, peaceful place where nature's gifts are endless and the creativity of its souls has no boundaries, you will have the peace of knowing that our loved ones are not missing out on life, they are living as sure as we are and are waiting to meet up with us again.

Let's be clear, however, that live is what we must do. We are living in a very turbulent time, and great purification is taking place in the world. Moment by moment, we do not know exactly how our personal journey will unfold or what will be required of us to help make our generation and future ones be able to know and recognize truth. All we have is now—the present moment, and a humble intention to do all that we can to make our lives contribute in a manner that God would be proud of. This earth is very important to God.

When we live and learn to place our humanness in proper context with our Maker, and we learn to honor life, nature, and God's light, we view things with greater humility and reverence. We began to understand that death of our bodies, whether it is in an accident, natural disaster, or old age, it is merely crossing over to the other side to fulfill a beautiful plan set in action by our Creator. We need to remember to be present in the here and now and honor life and live with graciousness in this ever-challenging world until God calls us home.

It is our responsibility to let go of limited ideas that keep us from experiencing life in the light. It is part of why we are here, to experience and learn the infinite circuit of life that connects us to the light so it can inspire our steps by enabling us to walk, to grow, to evolve, and to find deeper spiritual capacities to love and to know our true selves. As long as we fear, we live in denial of the light.

Do not fear to live even though you are in pain. Do not fear to be happy because you were created to be happy. Do not fear that you are alone because you are not. Do not fear that we end because we do not.

I would encourage you to live your life loving more, creating more, and sharing more of yourself, your talents, and your compassion. All these things will add to the heightened joy you will feel when the time comes for you to have your reunion with all your loved ones.

In the Beatitudes, we read: Blessed are the poor in spirit: for theirs is the kingdom of heaven. Blessed are they that mourn: for they shall be comforted. Blessed are the meek: for they shall inherit the earth.

Be diligent and courageous in hanging on because time will move more quickly than you know and you will become stronger, wiser, and more powerful than you can imagine. The rewards for living a good earth life are limitless.

When God's time for you has come to progress to the other side, picture your friends and loved ones embracing you and feeling proud that you did the best you could with the life you were given. They will rejoice with you! Can you imagine anything greater?

Beautiful is the light
That reveals truth.
Courageous is the heart,
That desires the light.
Straight is the road
That follows the light
Love is the intention
That makes everything right.

What I Know

W e haven't graduated from earth school until we take our last breath, so to be anxiously engaged in learning from our experiences and valuing the lessons that will hopefully earn us our diplomas is a constant until God decides differently. So far, what I know is: God is our light; he is the compass that will lead us back to our full potential, to our joy, and to all knowing. He created us in his image; this is why we call him Father. He doesn't care what path leads us back to him because there are many, he just cares that we come back. I know he loves us. God is absolutely pure love. He made the world we live in, and he made the ability to freely choose our path. People come in all different shapes, sizes, and colors. He made this purposely so we could learn tolerance and acceptance because what is visual to the human eye is not visible to the soul unless we are standing in God's light. If our eyes were closed and we extended our arm and touched one of our brothers or sisters, we would not be able to feel the difference, only that they are a child of God. How else can God get the message out to his children that what is on the inside is what he loves? God isn't so concerned about how you find him only that you do. When you seek and find him, he will direct your paths.

If you do not have love and charity in your hearts for others, sitting in a pew on Sunday will not make you know him. If you would like to know if the scriptures are true and understand what you read, ask him, he is the giver of wisdom, and he asks only that you learn to ask. God is not on the corner, screaming at the top of his lungs to accept him or you will be punished in hell. He is within—gently and lovingly teaching you to hear him so your life and your heart may have his peace.

God knows that no one arrives here perfectly wise, but all are capable of wisdom. Everything we do is an unfolding of his plan and purpose.

He knows the longer we live on earth, our beauty continues to progress inward. He desires that we know who we are, his children, and that we have patience when seeking his light, and learn how to give and receive love, for it will complete our life. He also knows that the person you are destined to become will be the one you decide to be.

What I also know is: children are precious and they are the future. They are one of our most sacred obligations. They come to us pure and un-blemished, like white parchment on which their achievements and aspi-rations of a lifetime are to be written. Whether their manuscript becomes a biography of love and honor or a series of smudges depends largely on the guiding influences in their lives.

Each one of us arrived here ready to learn and preparing to return. We are entrusted with divine stewardship over little children to help them grow so they may know who they are and that they are a living divine work in progress. We must love and respect them and never dare to tres-pass, step on or blow out the flame of pure love they arrived with. It is our responsibility to look into their eyes and see the sparkle of their divinity.

I recall standing in my crib. The memory is crystal clear, and now that I have command of language, I can interpret my feelings. I have just learned how to hoist myself up and hold on to the rail. I am jubilant for this feat and I am bouncing with excitement because I know Mom in her black skirt and crisp white blouse is coming into the dark room to pick me up. I am about ten months old, yet I remember the smell of her red lipstick as she nears me and I like it. It smells like love. It makes her nearness im-portant for I feel like I belong to her—I know I belong to her! My father walks in the room and makes a gesture that it is time to go. Mom holds me tight as my head rests on her shoulder. I know I will be going with them, Dad will be driving, and I will stand between them as we travel in the darkness. I know Dad is driving Mom to work, and I have already made up my mind that I am going to cry when he drops her off. I remember that night, but more importantly, I remember my thoughts. I was more uncertain about things at eighteen when I left home than I was when I was a newcomer to earth. I felt loved.

I have isolated that memory and it always comes to mind when I think of how quick this life races by. I'm not a baby in a crib, my mother and the smell of her lipstick is but a memory, but somehow, I am the same. I am that soul that stood observing with wonder everything that was part of my existence. I have forgotten many things in my life, but not how love was a fundamental part of who I was, even as a baby who did not understand the human language, I understood the spiritual feelings that love produced. I recall things that made me feel loved, like arms waiting at the bottom of the slide to catch me, arms tucking me in at night, or a smile on someone's face when they saw me and especially a kiss from Mom's red lips before she and Dad would go out for the evening. Kindness and tenderness made me feel loved, but always, love whispered familiarity.

I know I came to earth with a veil across my memory, but the memory of love was not curtained off because I've always had it. It is something we arrive with and are allowed to keep because we are to cultivate it, like a little seed in a garden, and make it grow while we are here. Love is receptive and recognizable to everyone's spirit, even when language is not present.

When my thoughts return to childhood, I recognize that the simple acts of kindness given to me by humble and reverent people were those that usually made a divine mark on my soul greater than anything else. Criticism and harsh words smudged it. Reverence embraces honor and gentility and consideration for others. It is respect for every creature and creation that God has given us. At the source of our true power and soul essence is reverence. Reverence is a sign of strength, and irreverence is one of the surest symptoms of weakness.

When we hold our little children close to our hearts, we are accepting that the unfolding of their life and their progression is necessary and sacred and should be held in reverent esteem for it is a noble calling we take upon ourselves. Reverence for some people must be nurtured and cultivated, and for some, they are born with it, but I know it should be a goal. It is conducive to accepting all of life and its inherent value. Reverence is a major conductor of the light. Reverence was one of the virtues that made President Lincoln great. His spirit of reverence was illuminated when he left Springfield, Illinois, to assume the presidency of the United States.

Before he boarded the train to leave, he turned to the townspeople who had come to bid him good-bye and in a humble trembling voice said:

My friends, no one not in my situation can appreciate my feelings of sadness at this parting. To this place and the kindness of these people I owe everything. I now leave, not knowing when or whether I shall ever return, with a task before me greater than that which rested on Washington. Without the assistance of that Divine Being that ever attended him I cannot succeed. But with that assistance I cannot fail. Trusting in Him who can go with me and remain with you, and be everywhere for good, let us confidently hope that all will yet be well. To His care commending you, as I hope in your prayers you will commend me, I bid you an affectionate farewell. 12

David O. McKay wrote:
"Reverence for God and sacred things are the chief characteristic of a great soul. Little men may succeed, but without reverence they can never be great."13

I also know that if you embrace reverence, you will embrace the beauty of the world. If you open your eyes wide and look around, you cannot help but see all the beautiful masterpieces of creation whether it is in the flowers, the deserts, the song birds, the waters, or the mountains, you will be filled with gladness. If we do not take notice, we are not truly living.

Mortal men have put a stigma on aging, as if somehow, we begin to depreciate like we are a piece of equipment we claim on our taxes. Because the body ages and movements slow down, they believe their creative useful contributions to society are no longer useful, valid, or necessary. To sit around in a rocker waiting for death is such a waste of the valuable time that can add to our continual progression. Why do we count our value in years? What is a year in the endless measurement of eternity? If we measure our value in time, the truth is that our time on earth may come and go, but eternal time has no beginning and no end.

As far as mortal life goes, each year, new souls arrive and other souls return home. So what then should we consider our greatest purpose as we age and mark off the passing years one by one? I know that it should be to cherish the attributes of our soul. Placing too much value on the things that are temporary diminishes the reason we came here in the first place and that is to develop a noble character, to increase love, reverence, and appreciation for all of life and God's creations. I know that I no longer care if I am tiny or if I have too many freckles. I do not look at people and decide their value by how they look. I'd rather look into their eyes to see if I can catch a glimmer of light.

After I have laid my mortal body down and the day comes when I am reunited with it in all its wonderful perfection, I am sure I will have greater knowledge and understanding of its value, but to allow my worth to be placed upon an imperfect temporary house, I refuse to accept that. God knows the content of each one of our hearts and that is where our stewardship begins and ends—in our hearts.

A wrinkled old man or woman can still enjoy sitting in a beautiful garden creating new tunes to sing and singing them. Wrinkled hands can still caress the brow of a tearful child or a grieving person. Even if we need a hearing aide, we can listen with concern as someone shares with us. As long as we are alive, we are still weaving the cloth that we take with us into eternity. As long as we have air in us, we are a creative individual still living to meet the goal of our life's purpose. Age or physical limitations do not remove any of our soul's essence, and that is the ability to give and receive love. Regardless of age, we can still have enthusiasm. Nothing great was ever accomplished without it. When we have enthusiasm, we are revving our powerful engines to drive us to success in whatever our undertaking should be.

Not long ago, I was standing in the checkout line at the supermarket. Behind me was a woman pushing a substantial- sized wheelchair for a man that appeared to be mentally and physically disabled. His head was secured tightly to a head rest, a belt secured his torso to the chair, and a large tray held his arms. He began making loud deep-throated gurgling noises that seized the attention of everyone close by. I could tell the woman was embarrassed because she tried frantically to quiet him down while looking apologetically at everyone. I turned to give her a reassuring smile that it was okay, but instead, I found myself looking at the man and smiling at him. When our eyes met, he let out a big squeal. It was, without a doubt, a happy squeal and a big smile crossed his face as he began to excitedly bounce up and down in his chair. I had never experienced such a magnificent response to one of my smiles in all of my years! It humbled me and confirmed what I already knew: the spirit has no limitations or boundaries when it comes to love. Bodies may be disabled and their command of language may be impeded, but the soul understands love as well as the pure love a child knows the day he arrives from heaven. Never underestimate the power of a smile either, especially a sincere one that reaches all the way to your eyes.

The love-driven person sees from a higher vantage point, much like what the angels see when they hover over the maze. You have a view of the bigger picture and can better understand how all of creation fits perfectly together, which is for the purpose of our evolution toward God. Seeing the bigger picture also helps give us compassion and patience for realizing that given everyone's individual conditions of their lives, most people are doing the best they can. Understanding this helps us see where we can be of service to those who are trying to find their path into the light. A sign of being in the light is having a sense of peace. Peace has been defined as the happy natural state of man. Without peace happiness is an elusive wish. Jesus said: "Blessed are the peacemakers, for they shall be called the children of God."

I know when it is difficult to find peace and comfort in the midst of our sorrows that prayer is an effective way to help us find our way back. Prayer is the yearning of the spirit to be able to speak the language with the Infinite Creator whose comfort and guidance is a never failing source.

I know that you cannot trust everything you hear or read or you cannot determine truth by vicariously living through the experience of another person. Sometimes, major falsehoods can start because it labels something by someone else's experience or perception. Personal experience is the true teacher of your truth. The way each person lives can determine the kind of experiences they will have. The law of attraction can give positive experiences or negative ones. How then do you trust something you hear to be true? It is wise to be very discerning. Consider the source from which it comes. Are you hearing from a love-centered high-consciousness being or from one that is unhappy and practices hurtful or fear-based behaviors?

I know that God exists. I believe there is not an intelligent person that does not recognize the existence of a power or force greater than himself, but can they know him as someone that can be invited into their lives or someone they can talk to or someone that can guide them when they are lost? I know because I have personally experienced it. How can you experience it? It requires a desire to know. Start with a simple prayer to steer you in that direction. It is quite simple. You can trust what the light will reveal. If you hear something from a reliable source, try practicing skillful faith, which means remaining open-minded enough to ask in faith and practice some cautious optimism until you can personally experience it within yourself. To know truth, it must be experienced.

The journey of self-discovery is meant to increase our capacity to recognize truth. Spiritual growth is like climbing stairs. Each new step represents a new stage of growth, a new awareness of what is true, and a purer understanding of what is beautiful and good. We have to be in shape to climb those stairs because it isn't always easy and it takes effort. As we climb, we shed our undeveloped identities and expand our higher conscious ones where the plan is to eventually arrive at oneness with each other and God. So as children who come to us with the pure innocence of God, we start with the essence of God's love and learn to magnify it countless times over so we can live in his light. That is why we should cherish children; they are pure and ready to embrace this life. They retain part of their memory of their preexistence, yet it must fade so that they may embrace their experiences here. It is part of their development. However, to understand them is to understand ourselves and the pure beginning we had.

In Matthew 18:3, we read: "Verily I say unto you, except ye be converted, and become as little children, ye shall not enter into the kingdom of heaven."

When you look into a child's eyes and witness a sparkle when he looks back at you, you are seeing pure accepting love. It is our responsibility to preserve it while also teaching them how to survive in this world, and it should be our goal to have that same sparkle emanate from our eyes. What do people see when they look at you? Do they see light? In order to develop empathy and compassion, children must learn to expand their world and their sense of connectedness and the same goes for all of us. Understand and appreciate children, and you will understand who you are.

I know that sometimes we find ourselves tried to the depths of our souls, which can stretch us to our breaking point, leaving us with raw and bleeding wounds, and many times, it may appear that there is no rhyme or reason why, but I know that trials work our patience and test our integrity. I also know that there are reasons why it is so.

World conditions and societal problems sometimes seem insurmountable. Even the universe and this earth have problems. Yet problems have a purpose. Problems exist to help us discover our soul. One of Abraham Lincoln's soul purposes was to oversee and correct an important human issue that was crucial for a nation born under the direction of a loving and fair God. So it is that trials teach us and it becomes our personal and moral obligation to discover our purpose so that we can make a contribution to the world we live in. Trials are never assigned to us to make us bitter, angry, or to promote hate. It is just the opposite.

I know that it is for each person to determine what they want their life story to read. This will require a look inside, not outside. This will require that you ask yourself—what are some of my unfulfilled desires? If you can imagine yourself witnessing your funeral, what would you want your story to say about you? You will be there, you know. It is not a quick, easy task. It won't come without soul-searching, motivation, and the hard work of application. It is a process. It is a journey of self-discovery. Start by creating a vision, a glance into your future the way you want it to be, and then let your thoughts lead you there. Believe in yourself regardless of what others believe about you. Be bold, for those who dare are usually the winners. When things go wrong, ask how you can learn from them, and then say to yourself it is just a speed bump in the road and move on.

Amazingly, when one discovers his soul's purpose, a key shift occurs. You begin to recognize events in your life as being teachers or you begin to see the sense they make. The good times as well as the bad are necessary in directing us in the right directions.

When writing your story, it will become evident that you are not only the writer, but the muse and the protagonist. You also see that the story flows better when you hire the best co-writer available—God. Just remember to be the hero of your story—because you are.

What I know is that our greatest purpose is to know how to live in the light while we are here. The light also gives us power to transform our lives. It helps us understand how powerful we can be when we rely on our authentic God-given senses. It tells us to lose ourselves in service to others for when we are in the service of others, we are God's agents. It tells us to be proud of our Godly heritage and strive to be the best that we can be, and it also tells us to love little children, to contribute to society, and to be nice and smile.

What I also know is the light tells us to knock down the walls that blind us from miracles and hope. I also know that when life gives us problems that we aren't prepared to handle, we can always seek help and ask for directions. When you ask, the light will show you many paths. I know that your loved ones that go before you want you to live your best life. They do not want you to prove anything to them. Every so often, blow them a kiss, talk to them, and send your love. They will receive it—without a doubt, and when they do, your act of love will make them smile—they ask for nothing more. And while you are here, you don't have to forget anything about them to be able to live again, and trust me you don't. Remember, love is eternal.

What I know is: if you want to know peace on earth, truly let it begin within your heart first. Begin by asking for the strength to let anger, hurt feelings, and conflicts end with you. When you enter a room, be the first to say hello and smile.

Another thing I know is that earth life is a mere fleeting moment. Before you know it, you are older and wondering where the time went. Someday is not a day and the time to forgive, be passionate, and start living your dreams is now.

Don't leave this earth without singing your songs, painting your masterpieces, or climbing that mountain. The longer you are on earth, the more beautiful and wiser your soul becomes. Do not let an aging body or wrinkles convince you that you have outlived your value or usefulness. Nothing could be further from the truth. The fact is your light shines brighter than ever. Before you know it, you will return home and you will either be proud of your choices or ashamed. Be proud! And by the way, call your mother, your children, and all the friends you wish would call you. Even if they have passed on to the other side, call them! This time, this day is your new day to love. It is quite simple—everything is within your power. I guess my mother was right: the light and everything that really matters is simply beautiful.

Endnotes

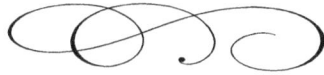

1 Graham, Stedman, "Diversity; Leaders Not Labels, Maya Angelou
   (2006), p.224
2 Lewis, C.S., Surprised by Joy, The Shape of My Early Life
   (Houghton Mifflin Harcourt 1995)
3 Roosevelt, Theodore, "Citizenship In A Republic"
   (Speech, Paris France, April 23, 1910)
4 Ramsay, David, The Life of George Washington
   (J. Jewett, 1832)
5 Wesley Hill, John,"Abraham Lincoln-Man of God
   (G.P. Putnam's sons, 1920)
6 Sparks, Jared, The Works of Benjamin Franklin
   (Whittemor Niles, And Hall 1856)
7 Khan, Hazrat Inayat, Mysticism of Sound
   (Pilgrims Publishing, 2002)
8 Dostoevsky,Fyodor,The Brothers Karamazov
   (Simon & Brown 2011)
9 Frank, Anne, The Diary of Anne Frank
   (Otto Frank 1947)
10 William Hutchison Murray's The Scottish Himalayan Expedition,
   J.M. Dent & Sons, 1951
   Murray, William Hutchison, The Scottish Himalayan Expedition
   (J.M. Dent & Sons, 1951)
11 Wolf, Gary, "The Next Insanely Great Thing" The Wired Interview
   (February 1996)
12 Lincoln, Abraham "Springfield Farewell Address"
   (February 11, 1861)
13 Mckay, David O., Secrets of a Happy Life
   (Book Craft 1967)

Biography

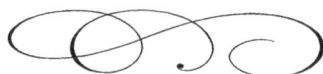

When tragedies or trials appear in our life, it may seem as if life is unfair and surviving them impossible. *A Legitimate Journey* chronicles Kathleen's story through such trials. Her lessons are many, and she desires to share them with others so they may find their way back to hope and happiness.

Our journey through trials is not easy and grief doesn't come with an instruction manual, but this book is the closet guide you will find to help you deal with many of those challenges. Kathleen also shares many valuable tools to help navigate the journey.

Kathleen spent many years working in the funeral industry observing many journeys of loss and healing. She also worked as a facilitator with the Compassionate Friends. As a public speaker and entertainer, one of her greatest joys is sharing the light and lessons of survival. She believes most people will face a mountain in their life, but she knows all are capable of making it to the top, however, to get to the top, you much climb it. Some of life's most profound lessons come while you are climbing and reaching the top changes how you view the world and your life.

www.ingramcontent.com/pod-product-compliance
Lightning Source LLC
Chambersburg PA
CBHW022006080426
42733CB00007B/488